Series / Number 07-050

MULTIPLE REGRESSION IN PRACTICE

WILLIAM D. BERRY
STANLEY FELDMAN
University of Kentucky

SAGE PUBLICATIONS
The International Professional Publishers
Newbury Park   London   New Delhi

For information:

 Sage Publications, Inc.
2455 Teller Road
Thousand Oaks, California 91320
E-mail: order@sagepub.com

Sage Publications Ltd.
6 Bonhill Street
London EC2A 4PU
United Kingdom

Sage Publications India Pvt. Ltd.
M-32 Market
Greater Kailash I
New Delhi 110 048 India

Printed in the United States of America

Library of Congress Catalog Card No. 85-050543

ISBN 978-0-8039-2054-5

08 09 10   17 16 15 14

| *Acquiring Editor:* | C. Deborah Laughton |
| *Editorial Assistant:* | Eileen Carr |

When citing a university paper, please use the proper form. Remember to cite the Sage University Paper series title and include paper number. One of the following formats can be adapted (depending on the style manual used):

(1) BERRY, W. D., & FELDMAN, S. (1985). *Multiple Regression in Practice.* Sage University Paper series on Quantitative Applications in the Social Sciences, 07-050. Newbury Park, CA: Sage.

OR

(2) Berry, W. D., & Feldman, S. (1985). *Multiple regression in practice.* (Sage University Paper series on Quantitative Applications in the Social Sciences, 07-050). Newbury Park, CA: Sage.

CONTENTS

Series Editor's Introduction

Multiple regression analysis is one of the most popular statistical estimation procedures in the social sciences. In response to this fact, we have already published two regression-related monographs in this series, *Applied Regression* by Michael Lewis-Beck and *Interpreting and Using Regression* by Christopher Achen. The former provides a basic introduction to the procedure whereas the latter examines how and under what circumstances regression is actually put to use in good social science research.

In *Multiple Regression in Practice*, William Berry and Stanley Feldman provide a systematic treatment of many of the major problems encountered in using regression analysis. Because it is likely that one or more of the assumptions of the regression model will be violated in a specific empirical analysis, the ability to know when problems exist and to take appropriate action helps to ensure the proper use of the procedure. Responding to this need for understanding, Berry and Feldman clearly and concisely discuss the consequences of violating the assumptions of the regression model, procedures for detecting when such violations exist, and strategies for dealing with these problems when they arise. The monograph thus takes the reader a long way in understanding the major problems posed—and potential solutions to those problems—when actually using multiple regression to test social science hypotheses.

In order to make the presentation as accessible as possible, the monograph was written without the use of matrix alegbra. And, whenever possible, the notation used is consistent with Lewis-Beck's *Applied Regression*. Because both the present volume and that by Achen assume a basic level of familiarity with regression analysis, they both make excellent companion and follow-up works to Lewis-Beck's introduction.

Berry and Feldman illustrate the problems facing researchers and the solutions they offer with numerous examples from political science, sociology, and economics. Because many applications of regression in the social sciences involve analysis of samples of cases randomly drawn

5

from a larger population, some of the major examples are constructed to show more clearly the properties of regression estimates derived from samples. Specifically, Berry and Feldman explain clearly the concepts of bias and efficiency in statistical estimation—key concepts that are often confusing to students. By making use of repeated sampling from a known population, the properties of sample estimators are much easier to understand.

In short, *Multiple Regression in Practice* should be a valuable aid for anyone making use of regression analysis in their research or anyone simply interested in understanding more fully this important statistical procedure.

—*Richard G. Niemi*
Series Co-Editor

Introduction

Multiple regression analysis is an important tool for social scientists in the analysis of nonexperimental data. When the assumptions of regression analysis are met, the coefficient estimates derived for a random sample will have many desirable properties. In the real world of research, however, one or more of these assumptions are likely to be violated. And when this occurs, the application of regression analysis may produce misleading or problematic coefficient estimates. If no useful results could be drawn when assumptions are violated, or no modifications of regression analysis could be made to deal with the violations, the attractiveness of multiple regression would be reduced significantly. Fortunately, there are means to detect when some of the assumptions are violated and procedures that can be employed to deal with the resulting problems. In Chapters 2 through 6 of this monograph, we will analyze the key assumptions of multiple regression analysis in a systematic manner. For each assumption, we will discuss the situations in which the assumption is likely to be violated, what effect violating the assumption has on the nature of coefficient estimates, how the violation can be detected in actual research, and what can be done to overcome the problems that result when the assumption is violated.

We will illustrate many of our points with examples. Because in most social science applications, regression analysis will be applied to a sample of cases from a population, we will frequently illustrate the properties of regression coefficient estimators by defining a "population" of cases and drawing a large number of random samples from this population. These examples will help show the problems that may arise when the coefficients of a regression equation are estimated from a single random sample. Although the "populations" so defined will be drawn from actual data sets, the cases will be selected to illustrate particular statistical issues. Thus, the substantive results presented in these illustrations should not be interpreted as necessarily representative of any "real-world" population.

We assume that readers of this monograph have had a prior introduction to regression analysis comparable to the level of Lewis-Beck's (1980) monograph, *Applied Regression: An Introduction*. Although we will present an introduction to the multiple regression model in Chapter 1, this is intended as a review of fundamentals and not as a complete intoduction to the subject. Because we are assuming nothing more than an introduction to multiple regression, we will not use matrix algebra in our presentation. We hope this will make our discussion of the application of the multiple regression model accessible to as many people as possible.

Acknowledgment

We would like to thank Steve Thomson for his assistance in designing computer programs to run regressions on repeated samples from a population; he saved us considerable time and effort. We are also indebted to Tse-min Lin for detection of an error in our discussion of the consequences of heteroscedasticity in an earlier printing.

—W.D.B. and S.F.

MULTIPLE REGRESSION IN PRACTICE

WILLIAM D. BERRY
Florida State University
STANLEY FELDMAN
SUNY at Stony Brook

1. THE MULTIPLE REGRESSION MODEL: A REVIEW

In the general form of the linear regression model, the dependent variable, Y, is assumed to be a function of a set of k independent variables—$X_1, X_2, X_3, \ldots, X_k$—in a population. To express the model in equation form, we use X_{ij} to denote the value of the jth observation of the variable X_i. The linear regression model assumes that for each set of values for the k independent variables ($X_{1j}, X_{2j}, \ldots, X_{kj}$) there is a distribution of Y_j values such that the mean of the distribution is on the surface represented by the equation

$$E(Y_j) = \alpha + \beta_1 X_{1j} + \beta_2 X_{2j} + \ldots + \beta_k X_{kj} \qquad [1.1]$$

where the Greek letter coefficient $\alpha, \beta_1, \beta_2, \ldots, \beta_k$ represent population parameters. The interpretation of these parameters is straightforward. β_i is called a *partial slope coefficient* as it is what mathematicians call the *slope* of the relationship between the independent variable X_i and the dependent variable Y holding all other independent variables constant. Put differently, β_i represents the change in E(Y) (the expected value of Y) associated with a one unit increase in X_i when all other independent variables in the model are held constant.[1] α, on the other hand, is called the *intercept*, and represents geometrically the value of E(Y) where the regression surface (or plane) crosses the Y axis, or subtantively, the expected value of Y when all the independent variables equal zero.

Each individual observation of Y_j is assumed to be determined by an equation containing an error term:

$$Y_j = \alpha + \beta_1 X_{1j} + \beta_2 X_{2j} + \ldots + \beta_k X_{kj} + \epsilon_j \qquad [1.2]$$

Thus, the error term ϵ_j is the deviation of the value of Y_j from the mean value of the distribution obtained by repeated observation of Y values for cases each with fixed values for each of the independent variables. This error term may be conceived as representing (1) the effects on Y of variables not explicitly included in the equation, and (2) a residual random element in the dependent variable.

For much of this monograph it will be unnecessary to specify the model in terms of a specific observation, so for ease of notation we will often drop the subscript, j. This leaves us with a population regression equation of

$$Y = \alpha + \beta_1 X_1 + \beta_2 X_2 + \ldots + \beta_k X_k + \epsilon \qquad [1.3]$$

$$= \alpha + \sum_{i=1}^{k} \beta_i X_i + \epsilon$$

Although implicit in the way the regression equation is written, we should note that it is assumed that the relationship between E(Y) and each X_i is *linear*, and that the effects of the k independent variables are *additive*. (A more detailed discussion of the meaning and implications of linearity and additivity is contained in Chapter 5.) In addition, several other assumptions must be met to be able to appropriately estimate the population parameters and conduct tests of statistical significance. They are as follows:

(1) All variables must be measured at the *interval level* and *without error*.

(2) For each set of values for the k independent variables (X_{1j}, $X_{2j}, \ldots, X_{kj}$), $E(\epsilon_j) = 0$ (i.e., the mean value of the error term is 0).

(3) For each set of values for the k independent variables, VAR (ϵ_j) = σ^2 (i.e., the variance of the error term is constant).

(4) For any two sets of values for the k independent variables, COV(ϵ_j, ϵ_h) = 0 (i.e., the error terms are uncorrelated; thus there is no autocorrelation).

(5) For each X_i, COV(X_i, ϵ) = 0 (i.e., each independent variable is uncorrelated with the error term).

(6) There is no *perfect collinearity*—no independent variable is perfectly linearly related to one or more of the other independent variables in the model.

(7) For each set of values for the k independent variables, ϵ_j is normally distributed.

These are the basic assumptions of the multiple regression model; problems associated with the violation of these assumptions will form the basis of the subsequent chapters of this monograph. The problem of measurement error (assumption 1) will be considered in Chapter 3. If the variance of the error term is not constant (assumption 3), one is faced with *heteroscedasticity*, discussed in Chapter 6. The violation of assumption 4—autocorrelation—is also considered in Chapter 6. When the independent variables are correlated with the error term (assumption 5), the result is *specification error*, which is dealt with in Chapter 2. The problem of multicollinearity (assumption 6) is discussed in Chapter 4.

Assumption 2 states that the mean value of the error term is zero. This should be of concern only when the analyst is interested in the precise value of the intercept. If this assumption is violated, the intercept is the only coefficient of the regression model that is affected. Finally, assumption 7 states that the error term must be normally distributed. This assumption is necessary *only* for tests of statistical significance; its violation will have no effect on the estimation of the parameters of the regression model. It is quite fortunate that normality is not required for estimation, because it is often very difficult to defend this assumption in practice. Furthermore, even to justify tests of significance, the normality assumption is critical only with *small* samples. In large samples, we can rely on the so-called *central limit theory* to ensure that even if the error term is not normally distributed in the population, the sampling distribution of a partial slope coefficient estimator will be normally distributed (see Hanushek and Jackson, 1977: 68). As Bohrnstedt and Carter (1971) have shown, regression analysis is quite robust against violations of normality and thus significance tests can be done in large samples even when this assumption cannot be justified substantively.

Parameter estimation. In most situations, we are not in a position to determine the population parameters directly; instead we must estimate their values using data from a finite *sample* (of size n) from the population. To distinguish it from the population regression equation, the sample regression model will be written as

$$Y_j = a + b_1 X_{1j} + b_2 X_{2j} + \ldots + b_k X_{kj} + e_j \qquad [1.4]$$

The most common way of estimating the values a and the b_i ($i = 1, 2, ..., k$) is to employ the *least squares* criterion—to use ordinary least squares (OLS) regression. To do this we find those values of a, b_1, b_2, ..., b_k that minimize the sum of the squared deviations of the observations, Y_j, from the predicted values of Y, $\hat{Y}_j$:

$$\sum_{j=1}^{n} (Y_j - \hat{Y}_j)^2 \qquad [1.5]$$

where

$$\hat{Y}_j = a + \sum_{i=1}^{k} b_i X_{ij} \qquad [1.6]$$

For the bivariate model with slope b_1 and intercept a,

$$Y = a + b_1 X_1 + e \qquad [1.7]$$

the value of b_1 that minimizes

$$\sum_{j=1}^{n} (Y_j - a - b_1 X_{1j})^2 \qquad [1.8]$$

can be shown to be

$$b_1 = \frac{\sum_{j=1}^{n} (X_{1j} - \bar{X}_1)(Y_j - \bar{Y})}{\sum_{j=1}^{n} (X_{1j} - \bar{X}_1)^2} = \frac{\sum_{j=1}^{n} x_j y_j}{\sum_{j=1}^{n} x_j^2} \qquad [1.9]$$

where $y_j = Y_j - \bar{Y}$ and $x_j = X_j - \bar{X}$. Once b_1 is known, a can be computed from

$$a = \bar{Y} - b_1 \bar{X} \qquad [1.10]$$

For the general case (with k independent variables), the formulas for the parameter estimators a, b_1, b_2, ..., b_k are sufficiently complicated to require matrix algebra (see Hanushek and Jackson, 1977, Chapter 5, for the general formula).

Sampling error. When estimating a population parameter from a sample it is important not only to derive a specific value, but also to estimate the effect of sampling error on the estimate. To accomplish this, it is necessary to consider the concept of a *sampling distribution* for a regression coefficient. This can be most easily understood as the distribution of the estimates of the regression coefficient that would result if samples of a given size were drawn repeatedly from the population and the coefficient calculated for each sample. Because coefficients estimated from random samples will deviate from population values by varying amounts, the estimates of the coefficients from a series of random samples of a population will not be identical, but instead will distribute themselves around a mean. The estimated standard deviation of the sampling distribution of a regression coefficient is known as a *standard error*, and is denoted by an "s" with a subscript of the regression coefficient of interest. In the bivariate case, the standard error of the slope coefficient estimator can be calculated by:

$$s_b = \sqrt{\frac{\sum\limits_{j=1}^{n} (Y_j - \hat{Y}_j)^2 / (n-2)}{\sum\limits_{j=1}^{n} (X_j - \bar{X})^2}} \qquad [1.11]$$

Extending this to the two variable case yields formulae for

$$s_{b_1} = \sqrt{\frac{\sum\limits_{j=1}^{n} (Y_j - \hat{Y}_j)^2 / (n-3)}{\sum\limits_{j=1}^{n} (X_{1j} - \bar{X}_1)^2 (1 - r^2_{X_1 X_2})}} \qquad [1.12]$$

$$s_{b_2} = \sqrt{\frac{\sum\limits_{j=1}^{n} (Y_j - \hat{Y}_j)^2 / (n-3)}{\sum\limits_{j=1}^{n} (X_{2j} - \bar{X}_2)^2 (1 - r^2_{X_1 X_2})}}$$

Finally, we can go one step further and derive a formula for the standard error of the partial slope coefficient estimator for a model with any number of independent variables:

$$s_{b_i} = \sqrt{\frac{\sum\limits_{j=1}^{n} (Y_j - \hat{Y}_j)^2}{\sum\limits_{j=1}^{n} (X_{ij} - \bar{X})^2 (1 - R_i^2)(n-k-1)}} \qquad [1.13]$$

where n is the sample size, k is the number of independent variables in the regression equation, and R_i^2 is the squared multiple correlation obtained by regressing X_i on all the other independent variables.

Looking at the component parts of equation 1.13 is helpful in understanding how the standard error of a partial slope coefficient varies. The term in the numerator of equation 1.13 shows that, all else being equal, the smaller the errors in predicting the dependent variable, the smaller will be the standard error. There are three terms in the denominator. The first shows that the larger the variance of the independent variable, the smaller will be the standard error. The second shows that as the multiple correlation between the independent variable and all other independent variables in the equation increases, the standard error will increase. Finally, for a specific number of independent variables, as the number of cases in the sample increases, the standard error will decrease. On the other hand, as the number of independent variables approaches the sample size, the standard error will increase rapidly.

Having derived estimators of the parameters in the regression model, we would also like to show that these particular estimators are in some definable sense "good" ones. This requires that we review some desirable properties of estimators. Two are particularly useful. First, we would like an estimator to be *unbiased*. An unbiased estimator is one whose mean over an infinite number of repeated samples is equal to the value of the population parameter to be estimated. This can be expressed more precisely:

$$\hat{\theta} \text{ is an unbiased estimate of } \theta \text{ if } E(\hat{\theta}) = \theta \qquad [1.14]$$

Unbiasedness is clearly a desirable property of an estimate of a regression coefficient. It tells us that *"on average"* our effort to estimate the population parameter will be accurate. However, it must be recognized that unbiasedness does *not* in any sense guarantee that any particular estimate of a regression coefficient will equal its population parameter. Because we have just seen that repeated sampling from a population will produce a distribution of estimates for a partial slope coefficient, b_i, all that unbiasedness does is to ensure that the mean of this distribution will equal β_i. Thus, in any particular sample, we can be sure that an unbiased estimate is no more likely to overestimate β_i than to underestimate it.

It should be clear from this discussion that unbiasedness is of little use if the sampling distribution of a regression coefficient estimator is very wide (i.e., the standard error of b_i is large). This leads us to the property of *efficiency*. All things being equal, we would like the variance of the sampling distribution of an estimator to be as small as possible. More precisely, b_i is considered to be an efficient estimator of β_i if b_i is unbiased, and s_{b_i} is smaller than the standard error of any other unbiased estimator of β_i.

An important result in multiple regression is the *Gauss-Markov* theorem, which proves that when assumptions 1-6 are met, the least squares estimators of regression parameters are *unbiased* and *efficient*. In shorthand, the least squares estimators are said to be BLUE: Best Linear Unbiased Estimators. The Gauss-Markov theorem does *not* guarantee that the least squares estimators that we have just derived will always be the best estimates of the population parameters. Most importantly, the theorem holds only when the assumptions of the regression model are met. If, for example, the true relationship between the dependent and independent variables is not linear, an alternative model will clearly give better estimates. Moreover, the Gauss-Markov theorem does not mean that the least squares estimators will have a smaller variance than any other estimator; it is possible that some *biased* estimators of the population parameter will have a smaller variance. Nevertheless, the Gauss-Markov theorem allows us to have considerable confidence in the least squares estimators.

Goodness-of-fit. Another issue we need to consider in this chapter is assessing the goodness-of-fit of the regression model. One popular statistic is R^2, which can be defined by the following formula:

$$R^2 = \frac{\sum_{j=1}^{n} (\hat{Y}_j - \bar{Y})^2}{\sum_{j=1}^{n} (Y_j - \bar{Y})^2} = 1 - \left(\frac{\sum_{j=1}^{n} (Y_j - \hat{Y}_j)^2}{\sum_{j=1}^{n} (Y_j - \bar{Y})^2} \right) \qquad [1.15]$$

R^2 will always vary between 0 and 1. It can be interpreted as the proportion of the original variance in Y that is "accounted for" by the regression equation. It can also be shown that R^2 is the square of the correlation between Y and the estimated values, $\hat{Y}$. It will reach its maximum value when $Y_j - \hat{Y}_j = 0$ for all observations j, and thus when the dependent variable is perfectly predicted by the regression equation.

A researcher should be careful to recognize the limitations of R^2 as a measure of goodness-of-fit (see Achen, 1982 for a general discussion). To begin with, it is very sample specific; regressions in two different samples may produce identical partial slope coefficients, but R^2 may differ considerably from one to the other due to differences in the variance of the dependent variable in the samples. Also, the use of R^2 can be misleading if one is trying to compare the relative goodness-of-fit of two regression models with differing numbers of independent variables. This is because R^2 will always increase (to some degree) when new variables are added to the equation, even when they may have no effect on the dependent variable. In fact, as the number of independent variables (k) gets close to the number of cases in the sample (n), R^2 will necessarily get close to 1.0. One way around this problem is to compute an "adjusted" R^2, defined as (Wonnacott and Wonnacott, 1979: 181)

$$\bar{R}^2 = \left(R^2 - \frac{k}{n-1} \right) \left(\frac{n-1}{n-k-1} \right)$$ [1.16]

Constructed this way, $\bar{R}^2$ can decrease when a new variable is added to regression model, even though R^2 will always increase. In the final analysis, however, the specification of a model should be determined by theoretical considerations rather than by rigidly following a rule of thumb based on an empirical measure of goodness-of-fit. (Another important goodness-of-fit statistic is the standard error of the estimate of Y, commonly denoted s_e; for a definition and discussion, see Lewis-Beck, 1980: 37-38.)

Hypothesis testing. Given that, most often, we are faced with the problem of estimating population parameters from a sample of data, we are not only interested in estimating a value for parameters, but in judging how likely it is that the estimates are close to the population parameters. This is most frequently done through tests of statistical significance. A test of statistical significance begins by establishing a *null hypothesis*: a specific guess about a parameter value in the population. In most cases, the null hypothesis will be that $\beta_i = 0$; the null hypothesis is tested against the alternative hypothesis that the regression coefficient is not zero. After the null hypothesis is chosen, a significance level must be established. This is the probability level, or degree of risk, at which one is willing to *reject* the null hypothesis. Finally, a test statistic is needed that can be compared against a known probability distribution. It can be shown (see Kmenta, 1971: 226) that

$$\frac{b_i - \beta_{i_0}}{s_{b_i}}$$ [1.17]

is distributed as Student's t, with n−1 degrees of freedom (where β_{i_0} is the value of β_i under the null hypothesis).

Another use of tests of statistical significance is to determine if the joint effects of *all* the independent variables on the dependent variable is significantly different from zero. Given a multiple regression equation with k independent variables, the null hypothesis is:

$$\beta_1 = \beta_2 = \ldots = \beta_k = 0 \qquad [1.18]$$

and the appropriate test statistic is the F value

$$F = \frac{R^2 / k}{(1 - R^2)/(n-k-1)} \qquad [1.19]$$

with k degrees of freedom in the numerator and n–k–1 in the denominator.

Finally, there are also times when it is of interest to test the null hypothesis that the joint effects of *several* of the k independent variables is zero (see Chapter 4). As will be shown later, it is possible for each of a series of independent variables to have nonsignificant partial slope coefficient estimates but for the combined effects of those variables to be statistically significant. More formally, if the regression model is:

$$Y = \alpha + \beta_1 X_1 + \beta_2 X_2 + \ldots +$$
$$\beta_k X_k + \beta_{k+1} X_{k+1} + \ldots + \beta_{k+r} X_{k+r} + \epsilon \qquad [1.20]$$

and the null hypothesis to be tested is:

$$\beta_{k+1} = \beta_{k+2} = \ldots = \beta_{k+r} = 0 \qquad [1.21]$$

then the appropriate test statistic is

$$F = \frac{(R^2 - R_m^2)/r}{(1 - R^2)/(n-k-r-1)} \qquad [1.22]$$

where R^2 is the squared multiple correlation coefficient for the full regression model 1.20, R_m^2 is the squared multiple correlation for the model in which the set of r independent variables $(X_{k+1}, X_{k+2}, \ldots, X_{k+r})$ has been deleted, and where there are r degrees of freedom in the numerator, and $(n-k-r-1)$ degrees of freedom in the denominator.

In this chapter we have briefly reviewed the multiple regression model. We have shown how the parameters of the model can be estimated, what the properties of those estimates are, and some ways of assessing the overall fit of the model. Although one of the chief virtues of OLS regression is that it can be shown to produce unbiased and efficient estimators, it must be recognized that these desirable properties are only obtained when the assumptions of the regression model are met *in full*. Yet, in specific applications it is likely that one or more of the assumptions will in fact be violated. In such cases, unbiasedness or efficiency may no longer hold. In the remainder of this monograph we will discuss the specific consequences of violating those assumptions, how these violations can be recognized, and what may be done to remedy the problems created.

2. SPECIFICATION ERROR

Specification error is actually a nice way of saying that the "wrong model" has been estimated. More precisely, we assume that in the population there is a specific way in which some set of independent variables, X_1 to X_k, influence a dependent variable, Y. Specification error can result in two ways. First, we may have the proper variables in the model but specify the *functional form* of the relationship improperly. The regression model assumes that the relationships between the independent variables and the dependent variable are both linear and additive. If these assumptions are violated, the least squares estimators will be biased. The second form of specification error occurs when one estimates a model with the wrong independent variables. Either one or more variables that should have been in the model are omitted, or one or more variables that should not have been included are, or both. In this chapter we will consider the effect of including the wrong independent variables in a regression model. The effects of nonlinearity and nonadditivity require their own treatment and will be dealt with in Chapter 6.

Consequences of Specification Error

The first case we will treat is the situation in which a researcher mistakenly includes in the regression model an independent variable that actually has no direct impact on the dependent variable. More specifically, suppose the "true" population model is

$$Y = \alpha + \beta_1 X_1 + \epsilon \qquad [2.1]$$

but that the model estimated is

$$Y = \alpha + \beta_1 X_1 + \beta_2 X_2 + \epsilon \qquad [2.2]$$

X_1 is therefore a *relevant* variable—actually present in the true model—but X_2 is an *irrelevant* variable, and should not be in the estimated model at all. What then happens to the least squares estimates if equation 2.1 is actually the true model? To begin with, it can easily be shown (see Rao and Miller, 1971: 58) that we will get an unbiased estimator of β_2. Given that in the population X_2 has no effect on Y, $\beta_2 = 0$. Thus, the expected value of the estimator b_2 is zero, so that $E(b_2) = 0$. Similarly, it is comforting to note that the estimator of β_1 from equation 2.2 is also unbiased, so that $E(b_1) = \beta_1$. Thus even with the inclusion of an irrelevant variable in the regression equation, the estimators of the critical independent variables are still unbiased.

As discussed in Chapter 1, however, unbiasedness is only one desirable property of estimators; we would also like them to have as narrow a sampling distribution as possible. It is therefore important to consider the impact of including an irrelevant variable on the standard errors of the estimated coefficients. The formulae for the standard errors of regression coefficients for equations with one and two independent variables were presented in Chapter 1 (equations 1.11 and 1.12). From these we can see, first of all, that even though when X_2 is an irrelevant variable $E(b_2) = 0$, b_2 has a *non-zero* standard error. The size of the standard error will depend on the variation in X_2 and the correlation between X_1 and X_2. From equation 1.12 we can see that the greater the value of $r_{X_1 X_2}$ and the smaller the variance of X_2 the greater will be the standard error of b_2. This means that even though over a very large number of samples, the average estimate of β_2 would be zero, in any *specific* sample we are likely to obtain a nonzero estimate. In other words, although unbiasedness guarantees that estimates of β_2 are no more likely to be greater than zero than less than zero, it does not ensure that individual sample estimates will equal zero exactly. Furthermore, even though most of these estimates will be small compared to the standard error of b_2, there is always some probability that a large value will occur simply by chance.

What about the standard error of b_1? By comparing equation 1.11 with equation 1.12 it can be seen that if X_1 and X_2 are correlated the standard error of b_1 will be greater when the irrelevant variable X_2 is included in the equation. The degree to which the standard error is inflated is directly related to the size of the correlation between the independent variables; the more highly correlated they are, the more the standard error of the relevant independent variable will be inflated. Thus, even though the expected value of b_2 is zero, and the estimate of b_1 is unbiased, the inclusion of an irrelevant variable that is correlated with a substantively important variable will reduce the efficiency of the estimate of the latter. This result can be extended directly to the case of more than one irrelevant variable mistakenly included in a regression equation. As can be seen from equation 1.13, the larger the degree to which the relevant variables are correlated with the irrelevant variables, the less efficient the estimates of the relevant variables will be. Thus, the inclusion of irrelevant variables in a regression equation can have serious effects on the estimation of other parameters of the model. The only exception to this is when the irrelevant variables are totally uncorrelated with the relevant independent variables; in this case, the estimated parameters will be unbiased *and* efficient.[2]

The second case in specification error occurs when a variable that *should* be included in the regression equation is left out. For example, suppose the "true" model in the population contains two relevant variables:

$$Y = \alpha + \beta_1 X_1 + \beta_2 X_2 + \epsilon \qquad [2.3]$$

An investigator may instead leave out X_2 and try to estimate

$$Y = \alpha + \beta_1 X_1 + \epsilon \qquad [2.4]$$

What does this do the estimator of β_1 and its standard error? The nature of this problem can be seen more clearly when it is recognized that if X_1 and X_2 are correlated, and X_2 is excluded from the equation, X_1 will necessarily be correlated with the error term. Because a major component of the error term in a regression equation is the set of factors or variables directly affecting Y that have not been included in the analysis, X_2 now becomes part of that set. If X_1 and X_2 are correlated, X_1 is correlated with the error term of equation 2.4. This violates one of the major assumptions of regression analysis as developed in Chapter 1: All independent variables must be uncorrelated with the error term. With this assumption violated, the Gauss-Markov theorem no longer guarantees that the OLS estimators of the parameters will be unbiased.

In fact, it can be shown (see Rao and Miller, 1971: 62) that the expected value of b_1 from equation 2.4 is no longer β_1. Instead,

$$E(b_1) = \beta_1 + \beta_2 b_{21} \qquad [2.5]$$

where b_{21} is the slope coefficient that would be obtained if X_2 were regressed on X_1. What we estimate then is not β_1, the parameter of interest, but a value different from that by an amount equal to the product of the effect of X_2 on Y in the population and the size of the relationship between X_2 and X_1 in the sample. This result can be extended in two ways. First, if there are other independent variables in the regression equation in addition to X_1 and X_2, for example,

$$Y = \alpha + \beta_1 X_1 + \beta_2 X_2 + \beta_3 X_3 + \ldots + \beta_k X_k + \epsilon \qquad [2.6]$$

and X_2 is left out of the equation when it is estimated, then the expected value of b_1 can be given as (see Rao and Miller, 1971: 62)

$$E(b_1) = \beta_1 + \beta_2 b_{21,3\ldots k} \qquad [2.7]$$

where $b_{21,3\ldots k}$ is the partial slope coefficient of X_1 in a regression in which X_2 is the dependent variable and all the other variables $X_3, X_4, \ldots, X_k$ are included as independent variables. And, if two or more variables that are correlated with X_1 are left out of the analysis, b_1 will be biased by the sum of a series of terms, each equal to the product of the regression coefficient for an excluded variable and the size of the relationship between the excluded variable and X_1 (Rao and Miller, 1971: 62).

What is happening when a relevant variable is excluded from the estimation of a regression model is that the variables left in the regression equation that are correlated with the excluded variable will pick up some of the impact of the excluded variable on Y. The result is biased estimators of those variables left in the equation. The *direction* of the bias (positive or negative) will depend on both the direction of the effect of the excluded variable on the dependent variable, and the direction of the relationship between the included and excluded variables. The *magnitude* of the bias depends directly on the relationship between the included and excluded variables: The more highly related the variables are, the greater will be the bias. This is also important because it shows that bias will only occur if the excluded variable is correlated with an included variable. Specification error will *not* be a problem if the included and excluded variables are independent; in this case, the estimates of partial slope coefficients for included variables are unaffected by the presence or absence of the excluded variables.

The effect of excluding a relevant variable on the standard errors of partial slope coefficients for included variables is oddly counterintuitive. Rather than inflating the standard error, excluding a variable from the equation will typically reduce the standard errors of estimates of the variables remaining. This occurs because the standard error of a coefficient tends to increase as the magnitude of its correlation with the other independent variables increases. Once more, note that the amount the standard errors decrease will depend upon how highly the excluded variable was correlated with the remaining variables. Of course, one should not take comfort in the fact that dropping a variable will improve the efficiency of the remaining estimates. The "improvement" is bought only at the price of biasing those estimates.

An Illustration of Specification Error:
Satisfaction with Life

In order to illustrate the effects of specification error we will consider the following model:

$$Y = \alpha + \beta_1 X_1 + \beta_2 X_2 + \beta_3 X_3 + \beta_4 X_4 + \beta_5 X_5 + \epsilon \qquad [2.8]$$

where the dependent variable (Y) is a summary measure of satisfaction with life (coded 1 to 20 with 20 indicating highest satisfaction), X_1 is family income in thousands of dollars, X_2 is a measure of occupational prestige (0 to 100), X_3 is years of education, X_4 is frequency of attendance at religious services, and X_5 is size of current residence coded in units of 100,000 population. As the "population" for the analysis we have drawn a subset of 665 cases from the 1978 General Social Survey of the National Opinion Research Center. Three of the independent variables in this model are highly intercorrelated ($r_{X_1 X_2} = .73$, $r_{X_1 X_3} = .57$, $r_{X_2 X_3} = .58$), whereas X_4 and X_5 are virtually uncorrelated with each other and with the other three independent variables. OLS regression shows that the coefficients for this model in the "population" are

$$Y = 10.51 + .065X_1 + .011X_2 + .116X_3 + .265X_4 - .056X_5 + \epsilon \qquad [2.9]$$

In this example we wish to demonstrate the effects of specification error in a sample of size 50. Although in most instances a researcher would have to be content with a single random sample, we drew 100 different random samples of size 50 in order to more clearly illustrate the effects of specification error on the unbiasedness and efficiency of OLS estimates. As noted in Chapter 1, if a coefficient estimator is unbiased, the mean value of the coefficient estimate over an *infinite* number of repeated random samples from the population equals the population coefficient *precisely*. Similarly, the mean value of the coefficient estimate over 100 random samples should be *approximately* equal to the population coefficient.

Part (i) of Table 2.1 shows the results of estimating equation 2.8 in the 100 samples. As can be seen, the means of the estimates of the partial slope coefficients across the samples (in column 2) do indeed come very close to the coefficients derived from the "population" (in column 1). Although the means of the estimates are almost exactly on target, the estimates from the 100 samples vary quite widely. In fact, for the samples of size 50, the standard deviation of the partial slope coefficient estimates for each independent variable is larger than the mean value of the coefficient estimates.

But suppose that instead of estimating equation 2.8, income (X_1) is left out the model and

$$Y = \alpha + \beta_2 X_2 + \beta_3 X_3 + \beta_4 X_4 + \beta_5 X_5 + \epsilon \qquad [2.10]$$

is estimated instead. Because X_1 is highly correlated with both X_2 and X_3, both of these variables should now be correlated with the error term of equation 2.10. Thus, the estimators for these two variables should be biased. On the other hand, X_4 and X_5 are only slightly correlated with X_1 so their estimators should not be substantially biased by the exclusion of X_1. The results of estimating this model in each of the 100 samples is shown in part (ii) of Table 2.1. The means of the estimated coefficients show that these expectations are correct. The mean estimate for β_2 (occupational prestige) is almost 3 times the corresponding population coefficient, and the mean estimate of β_3 is inflated by 40 percent. On the other hand, the mean estimates for β_4 and β_5 are still very close to their corresponding population values.

Finally, let us consider the effects of estimating a model with X_4 excluded:

$$Y = \alpha + \beta_1 X_1 + \beta_2 X_2 + \beta_3 X_3 + \beta_5 X_5 + \epsilon \qquad [2.11]$$

In this case, the excluded variable, X_4, is virtually uncorrelated with the other four independent variables so the estimates of these parameters should not be affected. Part (iii) of Table 2.1 shows that this is exactly the case. Even though X_4 is very clearly an important predictor of Y, its exclusion from the model does not cause the mean value of the partial slope coefficient estimates of the other independent variables to deviate substantially from their corresponding population values. These two examples show quite clearly that the impact of specification error

TABLE 2.1

Summary of Results for OLS Regressions for Equations (i) 2.8, (ii) 2.10, and (iii) 2.11 for 100 Different Random Samples of Size 50

	Coefficient	(1) Population Value	(2) Average OLS Estimate	(3) Column 2 / Column 1	(4) Minimum OLS Estimate	(5) Maximum OLS Estimate	(6) Standard Deviation of OLS Estimates
(i)	α	10.51	10.82	1.03	5.73	24.71	3.01
	β_1	.065	.063	.97	−.260	.485	.140
	β_2	.011	.010	.95	−.189	.172	.078
	β_3	.116	.119	1.03	−.527	.804	.254
	β_4	.265	.256	.97	−.437	.797	.265
	β_5	−.056	−.058	1.04	−.408	.128	.085
(ii)	α	10.51	16.60	1.58	8.24	23.95	2.58
	β_2	.011	.031	2.82	−.116	.178	.056
	β_3	.116	.162	1.40	−.306	.724	.186
	β_4	.265	.255	.96	−.440	.799	.234
	β_5	−.056	−.054	.96	−.370	.076	.073
(iii)	α	10.51	15.13	1.44	6.32	23.34	2.94
	β_1	.065	.063	.97	−.248	.484	.140
	β_2	.011	.012	1.09	−.202	.171	.077
	β_3	.116	.112	.97	−.513	.787	.250
	β_5	−.056	−.056	1.00	−.367	.111	.080

NOTE: Population values are from equation 2.9.

depends upon the relationships between the excluded variables and those left in the model. Where the correlation is high, the included variables become correlated with the error term and the estimates of their parameters become badly biased.

Detecting and Dealing with Specification Error

The most important thing to recognize about specification error is that, to a substantial degree, it cannot be dealt with at the level of data analysis. Specification error is at heart a question of whether the regression equation corresponds to the process being modeled and estimated. This means that an investigator needs a sufficiently well-developed theory to know which variables should be in the equation and a set of indicators that measure those variables. In particular, there is no clear-cut way of knowing, after the fact, that a substantively important variable has been excluded from the analysis. At first glance, it might seem that a low R^2 is a dead give away of specification error. It is tempting to argue that the reason there is so much variance in the dependent variable left to be explained is that important independent variables have been left out. Although in many cases this may be true, a low R^2 does *not* necessarily indicate that theoretically relevant independent variables have been excluded. At least two other factors may also contribute to a low explained variance: There may be substantial amounts of measurement error in the variables (see Chapter 3) or the functional form of the equation may be misspecified (see Chapter 6). As will be seen, both of these problems will contribute to a low R^2 and, therefore, the meaning of low goodness-of-fit is at best ambiguous. The only sure way to demonstrate the existence of an excluded variable is for a theory to point to the relevant variable that may then be measured and added to the empirical analysis.

Statistical techniques are a bit more helpful in detecting irrelevant included variables. It was previously shown that the expected value of the partial slope coefficients of irrelevant variables is zero. However, because the standard error of the coefficient will not be zero, a nonzero parameter estimate will usually be obtained. In most cases, however, the estimate will be small with respect to its standard error and a test of statistical significance will fail to reject the null hypothesis that the population parameter equals zero. But again, some care must be exercised before concluding that a variable with a nonsignificant partial slope coefficient is an irrelevant variable. As will be seen, factors such as measurement error and multicollinearity can also lead to a coefficient that is small with respect to its standard error. Rao and Miller (1971) suggest that a somewhat more sensitive test is to examine the adjusted explained variance, $\overline{R}^2$. If this does not decrease when the variable in quesiton is removed from the equation, it is clearly not playing any role in reducing the error variance and would therefore seem to be irrelevant. In addition, if a variable is truly irrelevant to the analysis, its removal should have no effect on the estimates of the variables remaining in the equation. As in the case of excluded variables, the best guide to whether a variable is irrelevant is theory. Even if all of the above criteria are met, a variable that seems to have theoretical significance should be retained in the analysis and not dropped for empirical reasons.

3. MEASUREMENT ERROR

Measurement error is one of the most important methodological problems facing the social sciences, and it can have a major impact on the estimation of regression coefficients in otherwise well-specified models. There is a tendency to think of measurement error as an all or nothing problem. This is very misleading, however. No measure is ever perfect; the question is how much error is present and what impact it will have on the analysis of the data.

What exactly is measurement error? Although a full discussion of this topic is beyond the scope of this monograph (see Carmines and Zeller, 1979), we can distinguish two types of measurement error: random and nonrandom. In both cases it is necessary to distinguish between *true variables* and *indicators*. A true variable is the theoretical concept we wish to measure. In many cases in the social sciences, the true variable will be unobservable—for example, people's attitudes and personality characteristics and nations' levels of economic development and democratization. Indicators, on the other hand, are the empirical observations we have made to measure the concepts. *Nonrandom measurement error* occurs when we are to some degree systematically measuring some other variable(s) in addition to the true variable of interest. This is fundamentally an issue of *validity*. Clearly, if the measures used in a multiple regression analysis are tapping variables other than those of interest, the coefficient estimates will be biased and very difficult to interpret. In this chapter, however, we will be dealing with the problem of *random measurement error*. Random measurement error is just that: error introduced into indicators that is unsystematic noise. Random error may be introduced into measures for any number of reasons. Where data is collected from human respondents, there may be guessing involved or the response categories may be vague or not well defined. In other cases, there may be errors in recording data, or even mistakes in coding and keypunching. More basically, random error may intrude because we are trying to measure an unobservable or abstract concept with a simple observable property.

More precisely, we can establish a measurement model in which the indicator (measured variable) is a function of the true variable and a random error term:

$$X_j^* = X_j + u_j \qquad [3.1]$$

where X^* is the indicator, X is the true variable, and u is the error term. In order to simplify things a bit, we can assume that the error term is "well behaved"; formally, the assumption of randomness of the error term means: u has a mean of zero $[E(u) = 0]$, is uncorrelated with $X [COV(X_j, u_j) = 0]$, and is also uncorrelated with the error term of the regression equation in which X is included $[COV(u_j, \epsilon_j) = 0]$. The *reliability* of a measure (denoted r_{XX}) is a ratio of the true score variance to the total variance of the indicator:

$$r_{XX} = \frac{s_X^2}{s_{X^*}^2} = \frac{s_X^2}{s_X^2 + s_u^2} \qquad [3.2]$$

More simply, the reliability of an indicator is the proportion of the variance of the indicator that reflects the true variable. A well-known result of measurement theory is that the presence of random measurement error substantially attenuates correlation coefficients (see Carmines and Zeller, 1979). We will show that random error has a substantial effect on multiple regression analysis that is less predictable than its effects on correlation coefficients.

Consequences of Measurement Error

The first question we deal with is: What happens when the dependent variable in a regression analysis is contaminated with random error? As can be easily shown, random error in the dependent variable is absorbed in the error term and increases the variance of the error term in the equation. Consider the following model:

$$Y = \alpha + \beta_1 X_1 + \beta_2 X_2 + \ldots + \beta_k X_k + \epsilon \qquad [3.3]$$

However, assume that instead of measuring Y, we have measured Y*, where

$$Y^* = Y + u \qquad [3.4]$$

In effect, then, we are really estimating

$$Y^* + u = a + b_1 X_1 + b_2 X_2 + \ldots + b_k X_k + e \qquad [3.5]$$

However, this can easily be reexpressed as

$$Y^* = a + b_1 X_1 + b_2 X_2 + \ldots + b_k X_k + (e - u) \qquad [3.6]$$

Because e and u are empirically indistinguishable (both are random error terms), and $VAR(e - u) = VAR(e) + VAR(u)$, the equation involving Y* will simply have a larger variance of the error than the equation involving Y. What will this do to the estimates from the equation? The most obvious result is that the explained variance R^2 will be lower as a result of measurement error in the dependent variable. On the other hand, because we have assumed that the measurement error in the dependent variable, u, is uncorrelated with the error term for the equation, ϵ, the partial slope coefficient estimators will remain unbiased. The estimators are, however, less efficient. Looking back at the formula for the standard error in equation 1.13 it can be seen that the standard error of b_i increases directly with increases in the error variance of the equation. Thus, even though the estimators of the partial slope coefficients from equation 3.6 are unbiased, their standard errors may be large and thus it will be more difficult for estimates to achieve statistical significance.

The situation is more complex when there is measurement error in one or more of the independent variables. Let us first consider the case of random measurement error in the independent variable of a bivariate regression equation. The equation we wish to estimate is

$$Y = \alpha + \beta X + \epsilon \qquad [3.7]$$

But instead of measuring X, we have X*, where

$$X^* = X + u \qquad [3.8]$$

In our sample, therefore, we are really estimating

$$Y = a + b X^* + e \qquad [3.9]$$

Given the assumptions we have made about the random error term, u, it can be shown that the *magnitude* of E(b) will be less than β. In particular,

$$E(b) = \beta \, \frac{s_X^2}{s_X^2 + s_u^2} \qquad [3.10]$$

Looking back to the formula for reliability in equation 3.2, it can be seen that with random error in X*, the expected value of b will be the product of β times the reliability of X* (r_{XX}):

$$E(b) = \beta r_{XX} \qquad [3.11]$$

This shows clearly how badly biased a bivariate regression coefficient estimator will be in the presence of random measurement error. Measures are often considered "good" in the social sciences when their reliability approaches the level of .8. Even in this case, however, the slope coefficient will be attenuated by 20 percent. As reliability declines to .5 we are estimating a regression coefficient that is half of the true value.

As we move from the bivariate to the multivariate case, the impact of measurement error in the independent variables becomes much more unpredictable. It is still possible to derive formulae for the expected values of the regression coefficients in terms of the true population parameters and the reliabilities of the variables. However, as Bohrnstedt and Carter (1971) have shown, in the multivariate case it is no longer assured that regression coefficient estimators will be attenuated in magnitude by random measurement error. Rather, depending on the reliabilities of the independent variables and the correlations among the variables, the coefficient estimators may be biased either upward or downward, and often by substantial amounts.

Although the formula for the estimator of the partial slope coefficient in the presence of measurement error for the general multivariate case is quite complex, it is useful to see the estimators for the partial slope coefficients in the case of two independent variables measured with random error. Assume we have the following model:

$$Y = \alpha + \beta_1 X_1 + \beta_2 X_2 + \epsilon \qquad [3.12]$$

But instead of measuring X_1 and X_2, we measure X_1^* and X_2^* where $X_1^* = X_1 + u_1$, $X_2^* = X_2 + u_2$, and where u_1 and u_2 represent random measurement error. As shown by Bornstedt and Carter (1971), the estimators can be expressed as

$$b_1 = \sqrt{\frac{s_Y^2}{s_{X_1}^2} \left[\frac{r_{X_2 X_2} r_{YX_2} - r_{YX_2} r_{X_1 X_2}}{r_{X_1 X_1} r_{X_2 X_2} - r_{X_1 X_2}^2} \right]}$$

[3.13]

$$b_2 = \sqrt{\frac{s_Y^2}{s_{X_2}^2} \left[\frac{r_{X_1 X_1} r_{YX_1} - r_{YX_1} r_{X_1 X_2}}{r_{X_1 X_1} r_{X_2 X_2} - r_{X_1 X_2}^2} \right]}$$

Even in the case of just two independent variables, the estimators for the partial slope coefficients can be seen to be a very complex function of the reliabilities of the independent variables and the correlations among the variables. Thus although it is at least possible in the bivariate case to know that the regression coefficient is being underestimated by some amount when there is measurement error, no such assurance is possible when estimating a multiple regression equation. And, in the multivariate case, the amount of bias due to random measurement error is not only a function of the reliabilities of the independent variables, but the correlations among them as well.

Where measurement error is present in an independent variable that is uncorrelated with all other independent variables in the model, the impact on the coefficient for that variable is exactly the same as the bivariate situation: The partial slope coefficient estimator is attenuated by an amount equal to 1 minus the reliability of that variable. Furthermore, the partial slope coefficient estimators for the other independent variables remain unbiased. In the most general situation, however, all one knows is that estimated regression coefficients will be biased when measurement error is present. The direction and magnitude of the bias is usually unpredictable.

One thing that is definitely predictable about the impact of measurement error is that it decreases the goodness-of-fit of the regression. This was demonstrated earlier in this chapter for measurement error in the dependent variable and it holds as well for error in the independent variables. A simple way to understand this is to see that measurement error generates a component of the variance of the variables in the equation that is random. Because random variation is unrelated to all other variables it will account for none of the variance in the dependent variable. Thus, even if a regression equation does not suffer from specification error, it is still possible to produce an R^2 that is considerably less than one because of measurement error in the variables.

An Illustration of Measurement Error:
Satisfaction with Life

In order to show some of the effects of measurement error on the coefficient estimates in multiple regression, we will again use the example introduced in the last chapter in which the dependent variable, Y, is satisfaction with life. Recall that there are five independent variables in the model, income (X_1), occupational prestige (X_2), education (X_3), attendance at religious services (X_4), and population size of current residence (X_5). As before, we will estimate the coefficients of each of the models in 100 random samples of size 50. In order to show the effects of random measurement error we have created two new variables: an indicator of income (X_1^*) and an indicator of attendance at religious services (X_4^*) both of which contain a random error component sufficient to produce reliability coefficients of .60 with respect to the original variables.

Let us first consider the case in which we estimate a model with the contaminated religion variable, X_4^*:

$$Y = a + b_1 X_1 + b_2 X_2 + b_3 X_3 + b_4 X_4^* + b_5 X_5 + e \qquad [3.14]$$

Recall from the last chapter that religion (X_4) is virtually uncorrelated with the other independent variables. Part (i) of Table 3.1 compares the results of estimating this equation in the 100 random samples to the population coefficients of equation 2.9. As is clear from a comparison of columns 1 and 2, the impact of the measurement error in X_4 is substantially restricted to the coefficient estimates for that variable. The mean value of the 100 estimates for β_4 is now reduced to 59 percent of its true value in equation 2.9. Because the reliability of the religion indicator is .60, this result is exactly what is expected as a consequence of equation 3.11. Thus when random measurement error is present in a variable that is uncorrelated with the other independent variables in a multiple regression equation, the effect is very similar to random error in the bivariate case: The parameter estimate is biased downward by an amount equal to the reliability of the variable. The estimates of the other partial slope coefficients, however, remain unbiased.

TABLE 3.1
Summary of Results for OLS Regressions for Equations (i) 3.14 and (ii) 3.15 for 100 Different Random Samples of Size 50

Coefficient	(1) Population Value for True Model	(2) Average OLS Estimate	(3) $\frac{\text{Column 2}}{\text{Column 1}}$	(4) Minimum OLS Estimate	(5) Maximum OLS Estimate	(6) Standard Deviation of OLS Estimates
(i)						
α	10.51	13.48	1.28	5.11	24.34	3.03
β_1	.065	.068	1.04	−.255	.539	.104
β_2	.011	.011	1.00	−.186	.174	.077
β_3	.116	.114	.98	−.581	.777	.253
β_4	.265	.157	.59	−.402	.634	.230
β_5	−.056	−.057	1.02	−.359	.125	.081
(ii)						
α	10.51	16.51	1.57	8.03	23.85	2.67
β_1	.065	.026	.40	−.231	.205	.084
β_2	.011	.025	2.27	−.118	.185	.065
β_3	.116	.149	1.28	−.433	.779	.247
β_4	.265	.257	.97	−.461	.802	.240
β_5	−.056	−.059	1.05	−.405	.117	.083

NOTE: Population values are from equation 2.9.

Now let us consider a model in which income (X_1) is measured with the contaminated indicator X_1^*:

$$Y = a + b_1 X_1^* + b_2 X_2 + b_3 X_3 + b_4 X_4 + b_5 X_5 + e \qquad [3.15]$$

This case differs from that examined in equation 3.14 as income is correlated substantially with both occupational prestige (X_2) and education (X_3). As can be seen in part (ii) of Table 3.1 the impact of measurement error in the income variable is very different from measurement error in the religion variable. Specifically, the average value of the 100 estimates of the partial slope coefficient for X_1 (in column 2) is now 40 percent of the population value (in column 1) even through the reliability of the measure is .60. In addition, the average estimates of the partial slope coefficients for X_2 and X_3 are both substantially off target; in this example, however, both these variables are measured *without error*. It should be clear, then, that random measurement error in a multiple regression model can have major effects on the estimation of the parameters.

Detecting Measurement Error

The appropriate time to investigate the presence of measurement error is *before* a regression equation is estimated. Once the coefficients for a regression equation have been estimated, there is no way of discovering whether or not measurement error has biased the estimates. But before a regression analysis is begun there are several procedures that can be used to detect measurement error; which is appropriate will depend upon the type of data that one is using. We do not have the space to discuss all of the relevant techniques here. Interested readers should consult a standard reference source on reliability assessment (see, for instance, Carmines and Zeller, 1979), or the literature on the use of multiple indicators of variables to detect measurement error of various sorts (see, for example, Sullivan and Feldman, 1979).

Dealing with Measurement Error

When still in the design stage of a research project the best advice that can be given for dealing with the problem of measurement error is to attempt to reduce it at the source. Strategies of data collection and coding should be designed to minimize the intrusion of random error. Where possible, multiple indicators of a concept should be collected so that estimates of measurement error can be obtained and scales constructed to produce more reliable measures (see McIver and Carmines, 1981). Of course, for those doing secondary data analyses, the number of indicators of a concept will usually be determined for the researcher. Moreover, even when great care is taken when collecting data and constructing indicators it will be impossible to completely eliminate random error from the variables. It is therefore important to know what can be done about the effects of measurement error at the data analysis stage.

As noted above, it is possible to derive estimators for the partial slope coefficients in a multivariate model in the presence of random measurement error if the reliabilities of all the variables are known. In this situation it is therefore possible to derive unbiased partial slope coefficient estimators by using the formulae of equation 3.13, or a more general formula for more independent variables with estimates of the reliabilities (see Johnston, 1972: 281-291). This is easier said than done, however. The formula for the partial slope coefficient in the presence of measurement error is complex and unwieldy with just a few independent variables. Also, although one can obtain unbiased estimators in this manner, computing standard errors for the resulting coefficient estimates is often a complex process (see Warren, White, and Fuller, 1974; Achen, 1978).

A more useful procedure for dealing with measurement error in multivariate regression equations is *instrumental variables*. An instrumental variable for an independent variable X_i is one that is correlated with X_i but has no effect on the dependent variable except an indirect effect through X_i. An instrumental variable thus has no *direct* effect on the dependent variable, nor is it correlated with any other independent variables not included in the regression equation. This in effect requires that the instrumental variable be uncorrelated with the error term in the regression equation. If one or more variables satisfying these conditions can be found and can be measured with little or no error, the instrumental variable(s) can be used to derive estimates of the partial regression coefficient that are unbiased in large samples. (Estimators that are unbiased in large samples are known as consistent estimators; see Kmenta, 1971: 162-171).

The logic of using instrumental variables is to derive an estimate of the partial slope coefficient β_i for the variable X_i purged of the random error component that is biasing the estimate. Assuming that the instrumental variable is unrelated to the random error term, we can use it to estimate the systematic component of X_i. Using this estimator in place of X_i^* in the regression equation provides a consistent estimator of the partial slope coefficient. In practice, this requires a two-stage regression analysis. In the first stage we regress X^*_i on the instrumental variable(s). From the results of this regression we then compute the predicted values, $\dot{X}^*_i$, and use this in the original regression equation in place of X^*_i. More formally, let us consider the general multivariate regression case where instead of measuring X_1 we have an indicator confounded by random measurement error, X^*_1. If Z is an instrumental variable for X^*_1, then first regress X^*_1 on Z:

$$X^*_1 = a + bZ + e \qquad [3.16]$$

The estimates from equation 3.16 are then used to generate predicted values, $\dot{X}^*_1$, for X^*_1, which are then used in place of the original indicator in the actual regression model:

$$Y = a + b_1 \dot{X}^*_1 + \sum_{i=2}^{k} b_i X_i + e \qquad [3.17]$$

If the conditions for an instrumental variable have been met by variable Z, equation 3.17 will provide a consistent estimate of the partial slope coefficient, β_1, as well as the coefficients for the other independent variables.

For an example of the use of instrumental variables to deal with measurement error we turn to a model estimated by Hanushek and Jackson (1977: 242). They estimated a three-independent variable model where the dependent variable is vote choice in the 1964 Presidential election (1 = Johnson, 0 = Goldwater),[3] X_1 is evaluations of perceived party positions for several issues, X_2 is party identification (on a scale from strong Republican to strong Democrat), and X_3 is party identification for those who were indifferent to the parties on the issues.[4] The estimates of this model using OLS were

$$\dot{Y} = .07 + .39X_1 + .61X_2 + .12X_3 \qquad [3.18]$$

Because there is reason to believe that the independent variables contain some degree of random measurement error, the estimates in equation 3.18 may be biased. To deal with this, Hanushek and Jackson (1977) needed to find instrumental variables for the three independent variables. This was accomplished by using a series of demographic variables and social background factors (income, religion, age, education, parental party identification, race, region of the country, and union membership). A strong argument can be made that these variables affect vote choice only through issue evaluations and party identification and therefore should be uncorrelated with the error term in the regression equation. Moreover, they should be measured with considerably less error than the three attitudinal variables in equation 3.18. Using the two-stage instrumental variables procedure, they reestimated the vote choice model with the following results:

$$\hat{Y} = -.07 + .90X_1 + .31X_2 + .26X_3 \qquad [3.19]$$

Comparing equation 3.18 with equation 3.19 shows that the estimates of the coefficients changed dramatically when the instrumental variables procedure was employed. The estimate of the effect of issue evaluations on vote choice was reduced by about 55 percent, although impact of party identification almost doubled. This again is suggestive of the impact that random measurement error can have on OLS estimates. (For other examples of the use of instrumental variables in dealing with measurement error, see McAdams, 1984).

Although the use of instrumental variables will provide unbiased estimators in large samples even when independent variables are contaminated by random measurement error, there are considerable problems in using this approach. First, it is often difficult to find appropriate instrumental variables in a particular analysis. The condition that the instrumental variable be related to X_i but not have a direct effect on the dependent variable except indirectly through X_i is very often hard to satisfy. Second, even if the appropriate instrumental variable(s) can be found, they must be measured with considerably *less* random error than the suspect independent variable or little will be gained. If the instrumental variables are measured with error, the two-stage procedure will simply substitute one source of random error for another.

A third problem with the instrumental variables procedure is that it tends to produce less efficient estimators of the partial slope coefficients. Thus, although this procedure will produce estimators that are unbiased in large samples, the standard errors of these estimates will be inflated. Moreover, it can be shown that the size of the standard errors will depend directly on the correlation between the independent variable and the instrumental variables. As the correlations decline, the standard error will increase (see Blalock et al., 1970). This means that for efficient estimation it is necessary to find instrumental variables that are as highly correlated as possible with the suspect independent variable. Finally, it is also important to consider what will happen if the instrumental variables procedure is used when the conditions for instrumental variables are not met. Blalock et al. (1970) have shown that when the instrumental variables are correlated with the error term in the regression equation, the instrumental variables estimator is often more badly biased than the OLS estimator with measurement error in the independent variable. Using instrumental variables to deal with the problem of measurement error can thus be risky unless there is a great deal of confidence in the assumptions that underlie the procedure.

An alternative way of dealing with the problem of measurement error when there are multiple measures of the variables in the analysis is the use of multiple indicator models. These models are able to take advantage of the information in the multiple measures of the variables to produce estimators of the coefficients of the model free from the effects of measurement error. These models can also be very flexible in dealing with both random and nonrandom measurement error. We do not have the space to develop the logic behind multiple indicator models here. Interested readers may consult Sullivan and Feldman (1979) and Long (1983) for an introduction to such models.

4. MULTICOLLINEARITY

In this chapter, we examine the problems created when multivariate regression analysis is characterized by multicollinearity. In doing so, we distinguish between *perfect collinearity* and less extreme forms of multicollinearity. Perfect collinearity exists when one of the independent variables in a regression equation is perfectly linearly related to one or more of the other independent variables in the equation. For example, in a model with four independent variables—X_1, X_2, X_3, and X_4—there would be perfect collinearity if

$$X_3 = (2.8)X_2 \qquad [4.1]$$

or

$$X_1 = (3.62)X_4 + (6.2)X_3 + 8 \qquad [4.2]$$

Alternatively, perfect collinearity is the situation in which there is some independent variable X_i that when regressed on the other independent variables in the model yields an R^2 of precisely 1.00. The reason these two definitions of perfect collinearity are equivalent is that this R^2 equals 1.00 if and only if X_i is perfectly linearly related to a subset of the remaining independent variables.

We saw in Chapter 1 that perfect collinearity violates the assumptions of the regression model. What, specifically, is the problem? In a nutshell, with perfect collinearity, the regression surface is not even defined, as there are an infinite number of surfaces that fit the observations equally well. We can illustrate this problem by looking at a graph of the case with two independent variables—X_1 and X_2. We assume that X_1 is linearly related to X_2 in a sample. For specificity, say $X_2 = (1.5)X_1 + 3$, as reflected in Figure 4.1(a). So instead of having observations for a range of points in the $X_1 - X_2$ plane, we only have observations for points on the $X_2 = (1.5)X_1 + 3$ line in the $X_1 - X_2$ plane. This means that all Y observations would fall on the vertical plane above this line, as sketched in Figure 4.1(b). And because all the points fall on this plane, we could use the least squares criterion to fit a line (denoted L) to the points, such that line L is contained in the vertical plane, as in Figure 4.1(b). But because regression analysis with two independent variables is equivalent to fitting a plane in three-dimensional space, we can see that a unique regression plane would not be defined in this situation. Indeed, any of the infinite number of planes which contain the fitted line L would fit the observations equally well. Two such planes (labeled 1 and 2) are sketched in Figure 4.1(c).

Thus, in the general case, with perfect collinearity among a set of observations, an infinite number of regression surfaces fit the observations equally well, and therefore, it is impossible to derive unique estimates of the intercept and partial slope coefficients for the regression equation. Fortunately, *perfect* collinearity is rarely found in social science research. Practically speaking, the only situation in which one risks perfect collinearity is with a very small data set. Indeed, one must avoid using regression analysis when the number of independent variables is *greater than or equal to* the number of cases in the sample, as such situations necessarily lead to perfect collinearity.

For the rest of this chapter, we assume that we are dealing with a less extreme case of multicollinearity—a case in which the independent variables in a regression equation are intercorrelated, but not perfectly. But before we examine the effects of "less than perfect" multicollinearity, several general points should be made. First, multicollinearity is a problem referring to correlated independent variables in a specific sample of data, and not in the overall population. If social scientists

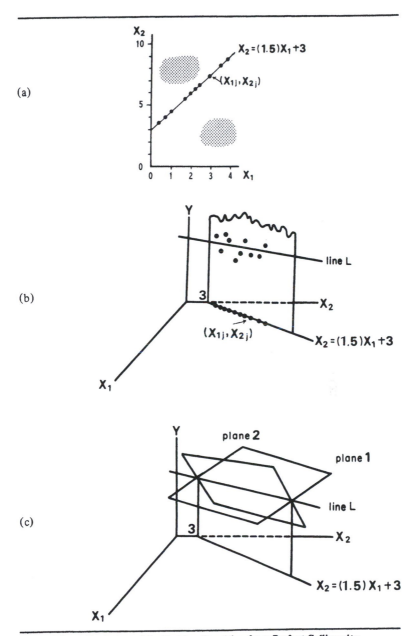

Figure 4.1: A Depiction of the Problem Resulting from Perfect Collinearity

could collect data using controlled experiments, the observations could be selected so that the independent variables would not be strongly related in the sample, and the multicollinearity problem would not be faced. Typically, however, such sampling is not possible, and thus independent variables may be highly correlated in a sample. Second, note that—setting aside the case of perfect collinearity—even a high degree of multicollinearity does *not* violate the assumptions of regression. The recognition that no assumptions are violated tells us that OLS slope coefficient estimators remain BLUE even when high multicollinearity is present. In particular, regression coefficient estimators are still *unbiased*. But multicollinearity poses other problems—problems that are the subject of the next section. Third, multicollinearity should not be conceived as something that either "exists" or "does not." Rather, multicollinearity exists in *degrees*, and the degree determines how important a problem is posed. When multicollinearity is present in only a very small amount, there is little reason to be concerned about its impact, but as the degree of multicollinearity increases, its consequences become more pernicious.

Consequences of Multicollinearity

We have seen that unless there is perfect collinearity in a data set, the assumptions of regression are not violated, and therefore OLS coefficient estimators remain unbiased, and in fact are still BLUE. Thus even with high multicollinearity, OLS coefficient estimators have minimum variance among the class of unbiased estimators. Unfortunately, with high multicollinearity, "minimum variance" does not mean *low* variance, as multicollinearity influences the variance of the estimated regression coefficients. We can see this by looking at the formula for calculating the standard error of the partial slope coefficient estimator in equation 1.13. The greater the correlation between independent variable X_i and the other independent variables (i.e., the greater the value of R_i^2), the smaller the value of the denominator in the formula, and thus the larger the value of the standard error of b_i. Thus, in general, the standard errors of regression coefficient estimators increase as the correlations among the independent variables increase. And this is quite plausible. Partial slope coefficients represent the effect of one independent variable on the dependent variable with all other variables held constant. But when the independent variables in an equation are highly correlated, it is impossible to separate out the effect of one—with all others held constant—with any degree of precision. In any event, because multicollinearity increases the standard errors of coefficient estimators, the major effect of multicollinearity is on significance tests and confidence intervals for regression coefficients. When high multicollinearity is present, confidence intervals for coefficients tend to be very wide, and t-statistics for significance tests tend to be very small.

The degree of concern that one should show for these consequences of multicollinearity depends on the purposes for which regression coefficients are being estimated. For example, if the major purpose of regression is to use information about cases having known values for a dependent variable to *predict* values for the dependent variable for observations with unknown values, the large standard errors resulting from high multicollinearity are generally of little consequence, as there is no need to separate out the independent effects of the correlated independent variables. Of course, if one expects the high degree of multicollinearity to disappear for the observations for which one will use the estimated regression coefficients for prediction, then the multicollinearity does pose problems.

If the goal of regression is *explanation* rather than *prediction*, the consequences of high multicollinearity are of more concern. But in some special situations, we can safely ignore multicollinearity even when explanation is the purpose. Consider, for instance, a model with three independent variables (X_1, X_2, and X_3), where r_{23} is close to 1.00 in value, but where r_{13} and r_{12} are both equal to zero. If our only interest is estimating β_1 (for X_1), the multicollinearity due to the high correlation between X_2 and X_3 would not cause problems. Estimates of β_2 and β_3 would vary considerably from one sample to another, but the larger variance for these estimators would not affect the variance of the estimator of β_1, as X_1 is completely uncorrelated with both X_2 and X_3. b_1 would have the same value whether we include both X_2 and X_3 in the model, or just one of X_2 and X_3. Note, however, that if we were to drop the assumption that X_1 is uncorrelated with X_2 and with X_3, the situation would change radically. In this case, the variance of b_1 would be larger as a result of the high correlation between X_2 and X_3.

Although large standard errors for coefficient estimators is a major consequence of multicollinearity, there is no guarantee that, if we find coefficient estimates with large standard errors, it is a consequence of multicollinearity. Indeed, there are several causes of high standard errors. They can result from a small sample for estimation, or from variables with small variances in the sample. Thus, researchers should avoid the temptation to capitalize on multicollinearity as an *excuse* for coefficients that are not statistically significant. Large standard errors *may* be caused by high multicollinearity, but might also be a result of other factors.

What distinguishes the impact of multicollinearity from that of a small sample, or from that of small variances for variables, is a second consequence of high multicollinearity—large *covariances* between coefficient estimators. In general, the larger the correlations among the independent variables in a regression equation, the larger the correlations among the *OLS partial slope coefficient estimators*. In fact, for a model with just two independent variables (X_1 and X_2), it turns out that the correlation between estimators b_1 and b_2 is $-r_{x_1 x_2}$, the inverse of the correlation between the two independent variables. Thus, we can see that when two independent variables in a regression equation are highly and *positively* correlated, their slope coefficient estimators are going to be highly and *negatively* correlated. When, for a given sample, b_1 is greater than β_1, b_2 will tend to be less than β_2; and when, for a different sample, b_1 is less than β_1, b_2 will tend to be greater than β_2. This, of course, implies that conclusions drawn about the relative impacts of the two independent variables on the dependent variable based on coefficient estimates from one sample are very shaky.

Detecting High Multicollinearity

Because—except for the extreme case of perfect collinearity—the issue is never one of multicollinearity either "existing" or "not existing," there are no tests that provide irrefutable evidence that multicollinearity is or is not a problem. But there are several warning signals that there may be a problem, and tests that provide information for making an informed judgment about the degree to which multicollinearity is present. One common warning signal that high multicollinearity is present is all individual partial slope coefficient estimates failing to be significantly different from zero, although the overall equation shows a good fit to the data. A common rule of thumb is that multicollinearity should be suspected when *none* of the t-ratios for the regression coefficients for independent variables is sufficiently large to indicate statistical significance at the .05 percent level, yet the F-statistic for the full model (equation 1.19) is significant. Furthermore, clues about the degree to which multicollinearity is a problem can also be obtained by examining the stability of coefficient estimates across different samples, or slightly different specifications of a model using the same sample. When high multicollinearity is present, switching samples, changing the indicator used to measure a variable in the regression model, or deleting or adding a variable to the equation can all lead to dramatic changes in the size of coefficient estimates. If any of these warning signals suggest that multicollinearity may be a problem, several more direct diagnostic tools can be used.

The most commonly used test for multicollinearity is the inspection of a matrix of bivariate correlations. Here one examines the correlations between all pairs of independent variables, and concludes that multicollinearity is not a problem if no correlation exceeds some predefined cutoff value—typically around .80. But this test is unsatisfactory for several reasons. First, it is possible that a severe multicollinearity problem may not be reflected in bivariate correlations; one independent variable may be approximately a linear combination of several other independent variables in the model, yet that variable may not be highly correlated with any other *single* independent variable. Second, it is very difficult to define a cutoff value that will always be appropriate. In some situations (e.g., with a very small sample) a single bivariate correlation among the independent variables of .70 could have very serious consequences for estimation, whereas with a larger sample, a correlation of .85 might pose fewer difficulties. Thus one always needs to look at the standard errors of slope coefficient estimates, the width of confidence intervals, and the purposes for which the analysis is being performed to assess how much of a problem multicollinearity poses.

A preferable test for multicollinearity can be developed by recognizing the meaning of perfect collinearity: a situation in which regressing one independent variable on the rest produces an R^2 of 1.00. The most reasonable test for multicollinearity is to regress each independent variable in the equation on *all other* independent variables, and look at the R^2s for these regressions; if any are close to 1.00, there is a high degree of multicollinearity present.[5] This test is superior to the examination of bivariate correlations, as the user will never mistakenly reject the possibility of severe multicollinearity because the pattern of intercorrelation is not reflected in the bivariate correlations. Also, when high multicollinearity turns out to be present, the R^2 technique clearly identifies the source of the problem, by pinpointing which independent variables are approximately linearly related to others. Unfortunately, using R^2s instead of bivariate correlations does not overcome the difficulty in defining how high the correlations must be before multicollinearity should be viewed as a source of concern; again, this will vary from one situation to the next.

An Illustration of Multicollinearity:
Satisfaction with Life

To show more clearly the problems associated with high levels of multicollinearity, we return to the illustration developed in Chapters 2 and 3. In this example (equation 2.8), a measure of satisfaction with life is predicted by five independent variables: income (X_1), occupational prestige (X_2), years of education (X_3), frequency of attendance at religious services (X_4), and population of current residence (X_5). As shown in Chapter 2, there are fairly high correlations in the population among three of the independent variables (X_1, X_2, and X_3) whereas X_4 and X_5 are relatively independent of each other and the other three independent variables. What are the effects of these large correlations when estimating partial slope coefficients from a sample?

We should first consider the detection of multicolinearity. Table 4.1 shows the bivariate correlations among the five independent variables for one of the 100 samples drawn. It is clear that income, occupational prestige, and education are highly correlated in this sample. However, the full magnitude of the multicollinearity is not apparent from the bivariate correlations. In the last column of the table, we show the R^2s from regressing each of the independent variables on the other four. An inspection of these coefficients shows how severe the multicollinearity is. Although the largest of the squared bivariate correlations among the five independent variables is .38 [= $(.62)^2$] the R^2 for occupational prestige (X_2) is .71, for income (X_1) .62, and for education (X_3) .56. On the other hand, less than 10 percent of the variance in religion (X_4) and population (X_5) is accounted for by the other four independent variables.

Although there is clearly a great deal of multicollinearity among X_1, X_2, and X_3, we have noted that multicollinearity does not bias the estimators of partial slope coefficients in a regression model. Thus if we were to estimate

$$Y = \alpha + \beta_1 X_1 + \beta_2 X_2 + \beta_3 X_3 + \beta_4 X_4 + \beta_5 X_5 + \epsilon \qquad [4.3]$$

in each of the 100 samples, the mean value of each parameter estimate should be very close to its corresponding population value. In fact, this was already demonstrated in part (i) of Table 2.1. This table shows that even in the presence of substantial multicollinearity, the average estimates of the partial slope coefficients (in column 2) are very close to the population values (in column 1). However, it is also apparent that the values of the parameter estimates vary considerably across the samples. In fact, for X_1, X_2, and X_3, the standard deviations of the 100 partial

TABLE 4.1

Bivariate Correlations Among the Five Independent Variables in
Equation 2.8 for a Single Random Sample, and R^2-Values when
Regressing Each Independent Variable on the Other Four

Variables	X_1	X_2	X_3	X_4	X_5	R^2
Income (X_1)	1.00					.62
Occupational prestige (X_2)	.62	1.00				.71
Education (X_3)	.54	.50	1.00			.56
Religious attendance (X_4)	.07	.12	.14	1.00		.06
Population (X_5)	.08	.17	.22	−.05	1.00	.09

slope coefficient estimates are more than twice the size of the corresponding population coefficients. This reflects the fact that in the presence of multicollinearity, although partial slope coefficient estimators remain unbiased, they are inefficient.

Moreover, as shown in Table 4.2, there are quite substantial negative correlations among the estimates of the partial slope coefficients across the 100 samples. In particular, there is a correlation of −.64 between the estimates for income (X_1) and occupational prestige (X_2)—a value expected given the high positive correlation between X_1 and X_2. This illustrates that not only are the estimators of the partial slope coefficients inefficient, but the deviations of individual estimates from the population values are systematic: When the estimate for income (b_1) in a sample is *larger* than the population value, the estimate for occupational prestige (b_2) in that sample tends to be *less than* the population value, and vice versa.

The effects of high multicollinearity can also be seen in parts (ii) and (iii) of Table 2.1. In part (ii), we estimated equation 4.3 in each of the 100 samples with one of the collinear variables, income (X_1), dropped from the model. Comparing column 6 in parts (i) and (ii) of the table shows that the standard deviations of the estimates for occupational prestige (X_2) and education (X_3) across the 100 samples are substantially reduced when income is dropped from the model. For example, the standard deviation of the estimate for β_3 is reduced 28 percent (from .254 to .186). On the other hand, the standard deviations of the estimates for religious service attendance (X_4) and population size (X_5) are largely unchanged when income is dropped. This again fits our expectations as both religious service attendance and population size are only slightly corre-

TABLE 4.2

Bivariate Correlations Among Estimates of Partial Slope Coefficients
for Equation 2.8 Across 100 Different Random Samples

Variables	b_1	b_2	b_3	b_4	b_5
Income (b_1)	1.00				
Occupational prestige (b_2)	−.64	1.00			
Educational (b_3)	−.41	−.37	1.00		
Religious attendance (b_4)	−.02	−.09	.07	1.00	
Population (b_5)	.04	.02	.03	.23	1.00

lated with income, and thus the standard errors of their partial slope coefficient estimators should be largely unaffected by the presence or absence of income in the equation. Finally, part (iii) of Table 2.1 shows the reestimates of the multiple regression model, this time with religious service attendance (X_4) dropped from the equation. A comparison of column 6 in parts (i) and (iii) shows that the deletion of X_4 has almost no effect on the standard deviations of the partial slope coefficient estimates for the other independent variables.

Dealing with Multicollinearity

If extreme multicollinearity is detected, what is to be done? Unfortunately, multicollinearity is a problem resulting from insufficient information in the sample, and short of increasing the information available, there are few reasonable courses left. Thus the best solution for multicollinearity is to *obtain more information*. If it is possible to increase the sample size, this certainly should be done. As can be seen from the formula for the standard error of the partial slope coefficient estimator in equation 1.13, when the sample size (n) is increased (while all other factors in the formula are held constant), the standard error decreases, thereby offsetting the effect of multicollinearity.

But note that increasing the sample size does not *always* result in a decrease in the standard error. In some situations, increasing the sample size might result in an increase in the correlations among the independent variables (and thus an increase in R_i^2 in equation 1.13). If this were the case, standard errors could wind up increasing with the larger sample. Thus, some new data are better than others for overcoming multicollinearity. New observations that have values for the independent variables that deviate from the approximate linear relationship among the independent variables are the best. For example, with multi-collinearity approximating the perfect linear relationship between X_1 and X_2 reflected in Figure 4.1(a), new observations in the shaded regions of the graph would be better than ones near the line $X_2 = (1.5)X_1 + 3$. In any event, although increasing the sample size is the best approach when high multicollinearity is present, it is not generally feasible. Presumably, an analyst would use all data available in the first place for estimating regression coefficients, and then if multicollinearity were a problem, there would be no additional data to which to turn.

A second alternative for increasing the amount of information (when no other observations can be added) is to use knowledge about the values of the regression coefficients themselves. For example, if one knows from prior research (or at least, one is willing to assume) that the population coefficients for two independent variables that are highly correlated have a particular ratio, it is possible to use this information to overcome extreme (even perfect) multicollinearity. Consider, for instance, the model

$$Y = \alpha + \beta_1 X_1 + \beta_2 X_2 + \epsilon \qquad [4.4]$$

where the independent variables have a sample correlation near (or even equal to) 1.00, but where previous research tells us that

$$\beta_1 / \beta_2 = c \qquad [4.5]$$

where c is a known constant. With this knowledge, we can substitute $c\beta_2$ for β_1 in equation 4.4, and obtain

$$Y = \alpha + C\beta_2 X_1 + \beta_2 X_2 + \epsilon \qquad [4.6]$$

This equation can be rewritten as

$$Y = \alpha + \beta_2 X_3 + \epsilon \qquad [4.7]$$

where

$$X_3 = cX_1 + X_2 \qquad [4.8]$$

Consequently, we can now use OLS regression to estimate the coefficients—α and β_2—of equation 4.7, where we calculate the X_3 values of observations by the formula in equation 4.8. Finally, the estimate of β_2 can be used along with equation 4.5 to derive an estimate for β_1.

Another situation in which we can use prior knowledge to overcome a multicollinearity problem is when we have a prior estimate of the partial slope coefficient for one or more independent variables in a regression model. For instance, with a two-independent variable model, where we have a reasonable estimate of the coefficient for X_1 from another source, we could use this information to help estimate the coefficient for X_2.[6] Of course, it is rare that we have reliable knowledge about either the ratio of two regression coefficients or the value of one or more coefficients. But if additional information in one form or another is not available, the possible options for dealing with multicollinearity are limited and generally unsatisfactory.

One of these options is to combine two or more independent variables that are highly correlated into a single variable—such as a weighted or unweighted average of the original variables—and then use the composite variable in place of the correlated variables in the regression. Unfortunately, this approach is only reasonable when the original model is *misspecified*. In other words, the approach is only appropriate when the variables combined into a composite are multiple indicators of the same underlying theoretical concept. Indeed, if they are multiple indicators, their composite is likely to be a more reliable indicator of the concept than any one indicator alone (Carmines and Zeller, 1979). But if the correlated independent variables are merely multiple indicators of the same concept, then the original regression model would have inappropriately included several variables representing the same concept, and thus the original model would be misspecified. In any event, unless the variables that are highly correlated can be viewed as indicators of the same theoretical concept, creating a composite variable to avoid high multicollinearity is not well advised.[7]

Another strategy commonly suggested as a way of overcoming multicollinearity is to delete from the equation the variable that is causing the problem. But if each variable in the original equation is an indicator of a distinct theoretical concept, it is a poor idea to delete any of the variables. The reason is that although it is a simple matter to remove a variable from a regression model, it is not so easy to delete the concept the variable is measuring from the theory underlying the regression. Assuming that the original model were well specified, the revised model would be *misspecified*. And, in general, the consequences of model misspecification—biased coefficient estimators—are more serious than

those of multicollinearity. Indeed, it turns out that the higher the correlations among the independent variables in a regression, the greater the
degree of estimator bias resulting from deleting a variable from the
model. We can see this easily in the two-independent variable case.
Chapter 2 shows that when the true equation is

$$Y = \alpha + \beta_1 X_1 + \beta_2 X_2 + \epsilon \qquad [4.9]$$

yet X_2 is left out of the estimation equation, the expected amount of bias
in the least squares estimator of β_1 is $\beta_2 b_{21}$ (see equation 2.5). But ceteris
paribus, the greater the correlation between X_1 and X_2, the greater the
value of b_{21}, and thus the greater the amount of expected bias. Consequently, in terms of the amount of bias created, the worst possible time
to delete a variable from an equation is precisely when that variable is
highly correlated with the other independent variables in the model. Of
course, in a perverse twist, this is the same time that the unsophisticated
analyst is most likely to delete a variable.

Given the shortcomings in these approaches for dealing with multicollinearity, on many occasions—when it is impossible to obtain more
information—the most reasonable course when faced with high multicollinearity is to recognize its presence, but live with its consequences.
Unfortunately, when multicollinearity is extreme, we must simply
accept that the data available do not contain sufficient information to
obtain estimates for individual regression coefficients that yield narrow
confidence intervals. One reasonable alternative in such situations is to
employ *joint hypothesis tests*, in which the null hypothesis would be that
the partial slope coefficients for all variables in a set of highly correlated
independent variables are zero. This test can be performed using the
F-statistic of equation 1.22, where $X_{k+1}, \ldots, X_{k+r}$ would represent the
highly correlated set of variables.

It is quite common in situations of extreme multicollinearity among a
set of variables that individual regression coefficient estimates may be
statistically insignificant, although the null hypothesis that all coefficients for the set of variables are equal to zero may be easily rejected.
This is illustrated in Figure 4.2. It contains a diagram of the typical
elliptical-shaped joint confidence interval for the partial slope coefficients in a model with two highly positively correlated independent
variables.[8] Note that this elliptical-shaped joint confidence interval does
not contain the origin of the graph. Thus, in this case, we would reject
the null hypothesis that *both* β_1 and β_2 equal zero. However, the

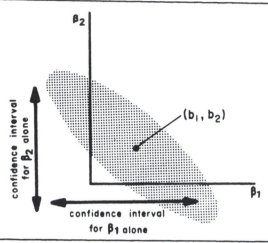

Figure 4.2: A Typical Joint Confidence Interval for the Partial Slope Coefficients for Two Highly Correlated Independent Variables X_1 and X_2

confidence intervals for the *individual* slope coefficients (marked next to the axes) both contain zero. Consequently, we could reject neither of the two separate null hypotheses: (i) $\beta_1 = 0$, and (ii) $\beta_2 = 0$.

We can illustrate the use of the joint hypothesis test with the model explaining satisfaction with life. Earlier in this chapter, we selected one of the 100 samples and showed that multicollinearity among income (X_1), occupational prestige (X_2), and education (X_3) is severe. Estimating the regression equation for this sample yields

$$\hat{Y} = 19.39 + .031X_1 + .008X_2 + .266X_3 + .324X_4 - .103X_5 \quad [4.10]$$
$$(2.46) \ (.089) \quad (.033) \quad (.240) \quad (.195) \quad (.057)$$

where the numbers in parentheses are the standard errors of the coefficient estimates. These standard errors indicate that none of the individual partial slope coefficient estimates are statistically significant at the .05 level. But the set of independent variables X_1, X_2, and X_3 are "jointly significant," as the F-test of formula 1.22 shows the null hypothesis that $\beta_1 = \beta_2 = \beta_3 = 0$ easily rejected at the .05 level. In this case, $R^2 = .24$, $r = 3$, $k = 2$, $n = 50$, $R_m^2 = .05$, and thus $F = 3.44$, with 3 degrees of freedom in the numerator and 44 in the denominator.

5. NONLINEARITY AND NONADDITIVITY

Recall that in the regression model, we assume that for each set of values for the k independent variables, $(X_{1j}, X_{2j}, \ldots, X_{kj})$, the mean of the distribution of Y_j falls on the surface

$$E(Y_j) = \alpha + \beta_1 X_{1j} + \beta_2 X_{2j} + \ldots + \beta_k X_{kj} \qquad [5.1]$$

The assumptions of *linearity* and *additivity* are both implicit in this specification. Linearity is the assumption that for each independent variable X_i, the amount of change in the mean value of Y associated with a unit increase in X_i, holding all other independent variables constant, is the same regardless of the level of X_i. In equation 5.1, this constant change is β_i—the partial slope coefficient for X_i. In contrast, if for any independent variable X_i in a model, the change in the mean value of Y associated with a unit increase in X_i varies with the value of X_i, we say that X_i is *nonlinearly* related to the dependent variable. Thus the relationship between X_i and Y sketched in Figure 5.1(a) is nonlinear, as the *slope* of the E(Y) curve [i.e., the ratio of the change in E(Y) to the change in X_i resulting from a small increase in X_i] varies depending on the level of X_i; a small increase in the value of X_i is associated with a larger increase in E(Y) when $X_i = 3.0$ than when $X_i = 5.0$.

The additivity assumption is also implicit in the assumption of the regression model that the means of the Y_j distributions fall on the surface of equation 5.1. Additivity is the assumption that for each independent variable X_i, the amount of change in E(Y) associated with a unit increase in X_i (holding all other independent variables constant) is the same regardless of the values of the other independent variables in the equation. Indeed, it is the assumption of additivity that allows us to interpret partial slope coefficients as representing the change in the expected value of Y associated with a unit increase in X_i *holding all other variables constant*, without specifying at *which* constant values the other independent variables are being held; the change in E(Y) is the same regardless. In contrast, if the slope of the relationship between X_i and E(Y) varies with the values of other independent variables, the model is called *nonadditive* or *interactive*. For example, in a model with independent variables X_1 and X_2, if the relationship between E(Y) and X_1 is reflected in Figure 5.1(b) by line 1 when $X_2 = 0$, by line 2 when $X_2 = 1$, and by line 3 when $X_2 = 4$, the model would be nonadditive.

The meanings of nonlinearity and nonadditivity are often confused, likely for two reasons. First, both nonlinearity and nonadditivity refer to a situation in which (contrary to the assumption of the regression

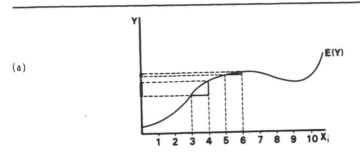

(a)

A Nonlinear Relationship Between X_i and $E(Y)$

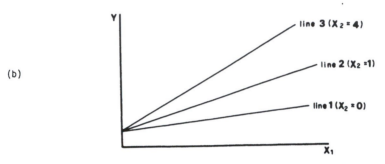

(b)

A Nonadditive Relationship in a Model With Independent Variables X_1 and X_2

Figure 5.1: Illustrations of Nonlinear and Nonadditive Models

model) the relationship between an independent variable and a dependent variable *varies* according to the *context*. So there is this similarity. But the similarity is limited, as with nonlinearity, the relationship between an independent variable and the dependent variable varies with the level of *that* independent variable; whereas with nonadditivity, the relationship between an independent variable and a dependent variable varies with the level of *other* independent variables.

A second reason for possible confusion is that similar techniques are generally used to modify the regression model to accommodate nonadditivity and nonlinearity. We will see that many nonlinear or nonadditive specifications can be converted to linear/additive form by performing transformations on the variables in the model. For example, if Y is related to X_1 by the equation

$$E(Y_j) = \alpha + \beta_1 X_{1j}^2 \qquad [5.2]$$

and the relationship between the variables is therefore nonlinear, we can define a new variable Z by $Z_j = X_{1j}^2$. Then, the new variable Z is linearly related to Y, and OLS regression analysis can be used to estimate the coefficients of the model. With equation 5.2, we say the relationship between X_1 and E(Y) is *nonlinear* in terms of the *variables*, but *linear* in terms of the *parameters*. And, indeed, there are numerous types of specifications that are nonlinear and/or nonadditive in terms of the variables, but both linear and additive in terms of the parameters. Given appropriate transformations of the variables, all these specifications can be converted into models for which coefficients can be estimated using OLS regression. This chapter will examine several of these specifications. Of course, there are an infinite number of alternative interactive and nonlinear specifications that are nonlinear or nonadditive in terms of both variables and *parameters*. Unfortunately, coefficients for such models can not be estimated using OLS regression even with preliminary transformations. Instead, maximum likelihood estimation procedures are needed—procedures that are beyond the scope of this monograph.[9]

Detecting Nonlinearity and Nonadditivity

The best way to detect both nonlinearity and nonadditivity is to use the theory underlying the model being developed to determine the hypothesized form of the nonlinear or nonadditive relationship, specify a model reflecting this form, and estimate its parameters; the statistics accompanying the regression then provide evidence about whether the hypothesis is true. The key question one must ask in deciding if there is reason to expect nonlinearity or nonadditivity is whether for each independent variable the slope of the relationship between the dependent variable and the independent variable can be expected to vary depending on the "context." If theory suggests, for example, that the ratio of the change in E(Y) associated with a small increase in X_1 depends on the value of X_1, a nonlinear specification is required. Similarly, if theory suggests that the change in E(Y) associated with a small increase in X_1 depends on the level of another independent variable, an interactive model is called for.

But the decision that a nonlinear or nonadditive specification is required is only the first step. The next question is what type of nonlinearity or interaction can be expected. With respect to nonlinearity in the relationship between X_1 and E(Y), questions like the following must be asked: Can the slope of the relationship between X_1 and E(Y) be expected to have the same *sign* for all values of X_1? If not, at what level of

X_1 can the sign be expected to switch from positive to negative? Should we expect the magnitude of the slope to increase as X_1 increases, or decrease as X_1 increases? Or perhaps as X_1 increases, the slope will increase over a certain range of X_1 values but decrease over other ranges. If the slope does increase over a range of X_1 values, does it increase at a greater, lesser, or steady rate as the level of X_1 increases? Indeed, an extremely useful technique when nonlinearity is expected is to use the answer to questions such as these to sketch the expected relationship between the dependent variable and each independable variable (holding all other independent variables constant) on graphs. Then once the expected relationships are clarified in this manner, an analyst can seek a mathematical specification that reflects them.

The same types of questions can be used to discern the form of the interaction expected. The only difference is that this time, we pose questions about how the slope of the relationship between an independent variable and the dependent variable can be expected to change as the values of other independent variables change. The answers to these questions alert us to the type of interaction expected; then we are in position to seek a mathematical equation that reflects this type. We stress, then, that the first step in detecting nonlinearity and nonadditivity should be *theoretical* rather than *technical*. Once the nature of the expected nonlinearity or nonadditivity is understood well enough to make a rough graph of its form, the technical work should begin. Later in this chapter, we examine several different kinds of mathematical specifications that can be used to model a variety of types of nonlinearity and nonadditivity.

But there are techniques that can be used to detect nonlinearity and nonadditivity even when the precise nature of the relationship can not be anticipated beforehand. For a bivariate model, the simplest initial test for nonlinearity is to examine a scatter diagram of the sample relationship between the independent and dependent variables. Sometimes, nonlinearity will be sufficiently striking so that it is clearly evident that the curve that best fits the points on the graph does not take the form of a line. However, a more rigorous test is available. This involves dividing the cases into several subsamples, where each subsample includes a range of values for the independent variable. Then, if regression on each subsample separately generates slope and intercept estimates that differ substantially across subsamples, the relationship between the two variables is nonlinear.

In fact, an equivalent test can be carried out with a single regression equation using dummy variables. Assume we have a sample of n cases, and wish to test for nonlinearity in the relationship between X and Y.

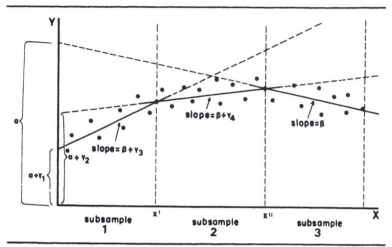

Figure 5.2: An Illustration of a Test for Nonlinearity

We could divide the sample into three subsamples as depicted in Figure 5.2. The subsamples consist of cases having X values in the three ranges: (1) less than X', (2) greater than X' but less than X'', and (3) greater than X''. Then, a test for nonlinearity could be performed by estimating coefficients for the regression model

$$Y_j = \alpha + \beta X_j + \gamma_1 Z_{1j} + \gamma_2 Z_{2j} + \gamma_3 (X_j Z_{1j}) + \gamma_4 (X_j Z_{2j}) + \epsilon_j \qquad [5.3]$$

where

$Z_{1j} = 1$ if observation j is in subsample 1, and 0 otherwise, and

$Z_{2j} = 1$ if observation j is in subsample 2, and 0 otherwise.

Note that for cases in subsample 1 (i.e., when $Z_{1j} = 1$ and $Z_{2j} = 0$), regression equation 5.3 reduces to

$$Y_j = \alpha + \beta X_j + \gamma_1 + \gamma_3 X_j + \epsilon_j$$

$$= (a + \gamma_1) + (\beta + \gamma_3) X_j + \epsilon_j \qquad [5.4]$$

For cases in subsample 2 (i.e., when $Z_{1j} = 0$ and $Z_{2j} = 1$), the regression equation becomes

$$Y_j = (\alpha + \gamma_2) + (\beta + \gamma_4) X_j + \epsilon_j \qquad [5.5]$$

Finally, for cases in subsample 3 (i.e., when $Z_{1j} = Z_{2j} = 0$), equation 5.3 reduces to

$$Y_j = \alpha + \beta X_j + \epsilon_j \qquad [5.6]$$

If the relationship between X and Y were linear (over the range of the three subsamples together), the slopes and intercepts for equations 5.4, 5.5, and 5.6 must be identical (in contrast to the nonlinear relationship depicted in Figure 5.2), and thus γ_1, γ_2, γ_3, and γ_4 must all equal 0. Thus a test of linearity can be performed by testing the null hypothesis

$$H_0 : \gamma_1 = \gamma_2 = \gamma_3 = \gamma_4 = 0 \qquad [5.7]$$

against the research hypothesis that H_0 is not true. The appropriate test of significance here is the F-statistic of formula 1.22, where R is the multiple correlation coefficient for full equation 5.3, R_m is the multiple correlation obtained when Y is regressed on X alone, r = 4, and k = 1. The F distribution has 4 degrees of freedom in the numerator and (n – 6) in the denominator.

Clearly, the choice to use three subsamples in the test for linearity was arbitrary, and the same type of test can be applied using any number of subsamples (less than n/3). In general, if the sample is divided into n_s subsamples, $n_s - 1$ dichotomous variables must be created, and $2(n_s - 1)$ terms will be included as independent variables in the test regression along with X. The formula for calculating the F-statistic for testing the null hypothesis of linearity is again an adaptation of formula 1.22, where R is the multiple correlation for the full regression equation, R_m is the multiple correlation for Y regressed on X, $r = 2(n_s - 1)$, and k = 1. Of course, the arbitrary nature of the choice about the number of sub-samples is a limitation of the technique, because the number selected can greatly influence whether the null hypothesis will be accepted or rejected. Indeed, when the sample size (n) is very *large*, and the sample is divided into a *large* number of *subsamples*, it is "very easy" to reject the null hypothesis of linearity. So when working with a large sample, an analyst must be careful to keep the number of subsamples established small enough so that the null hypothesis will not be rejected when the degree of deviation from linearity is substantively trivial. However, when working with a sample *small* enough so that n_s is large relative to n, it is "extremely difficult" to reject the null hypothesis of linearity, and a test may fail to reject "linearity" even when there are substantively meaningful shifts in the slope of the relationship between X and E(Y) over the range of X.

The same procedure can be modified to test for nonadditivity. For instance, assume we want to test the null hypothesis that the independent variables X and X_2 have additive effects on Y. We would divide our sample into subsamples based on the values of the cases for one of the independent variables—say X_2—and run regression on a model containing the independent variable X and terms including dichotomous variables based on the values of X_2. Indeed, if three subsamples are used, equation 5.3 would be the test regression model estimated, and the null hypothesis expressed as equation 5.7 would be the hypothesis of no interaction between X and X_2. Equation 1.22 would also hold as the formula for calculating the F-statistic for the test of significance.

Dealing with Nonlinearity

When the analyst is convinced—based on theoretical or empirical evidence—that relationships among variables in the model being examined are nonlinear, attention must focus on finding a mathematical specification consistent with the type of nonlinearity expected. Most of the infinite number of nonlinear specifications are nonlinear in terms of both variables and parameters—and thus can only be reasonably estimated using maximum likelihood procedures. But there are a variety of nonlinear specifications that are linear in terms of *parameters*, and for which OLS regression can be used following an appropriate transformation of the original equation. There are such specifications for models in which the slope of the relationship between X and E(Y) changes sign one or more times as the value of X increases. There are also specifications that assume the slope of the relationship between X and E(Y) maintains the same sign but either increases or decreases in magnitude as X increases.

The polynomial model. One nonlinear specification that is linear in terms of parameters is the *polynomial* model. It is appropriate for models in which the slope of the relationship between an independent variable X_1 and E(Y) is thought to change sign as the value of X_1 increases. For many such models, the relationship between X_1 and Y can be accurately reflected with a specification in which Y is viewed as a function of X_1 and one or more *powers* of X_1, as in

$$Y = \alpha + \beta_1 X_1 + \beta_2 X_1^2 + \beta_3 X_1^3 + \ldots + \beta_m X_1^m + \epsilon \qquad [5.8]$$

where m is referred to as the *order* of the equation, and is an integer greater than 1. The graph of the relationship between X_1 and $E(Y)$ expressed by this equation consists of a curve with one or more "bends," points at which the slope of the curve changes sign. The number of bends in the curve is determined by the order of the equation. Indeed, the number of bends nearly always equals m – 1.[10] Thus, a polynomial model for m = 2 generally takes the form of the graph in Figure 5.3(a), while one for m = 3 typically looks like the graph in Figure 5.3(b).

The parameters of model 5.8 can easily be estimated by defining the powers of X_1 as distinct variables, in essence, letting $X_{2j} = X_{1j}^2$, $X_{3j} = X_{1j}^3, \ldots,$ and $X_{mj} = X_{1j}^m$. Then OLS regression can be applied to the equation

$$Y = \alpha + \beta_1 X_1 + \beta_2 X_2 + \ldots + \beta_m X_m + \epsilon \qquad [5.9]$$

Several comments about polynomial models are in order. First, note that the independent variables in equation 5.9 are each mathematically defined as functions of a single *conceptual* variable. Because these variables are not *linearly* related, the analyst need not worry about *perfect* collinearity. But nonetheless, it is possible that the independent variables could be highly correlated. So when employing a polynomial model, it is wise to check for multicollinearity using the techniques presented in Chapter 4. Second, note that one can modify the specification of equation 5.8 to accommodate multiple *conceptual* variables. For example, one can include a second conceptual variable that is assumed to be *linearly* related to $E(Y)$ by adding an independent variable X_2 to equation 5.8, or a second conceptual variable that is assumed to be *nonlinearly* related to Y by adding terms for X_2 and one or more of its powers. Finally, the analyst must be careful in interpreting the estimated coefficients for polynomial models. The typical interpretation of a partial slope coefficient as representing the change in $E(Y)$ associated with a unit increase in an independent variable when all other variables are held constant makes no sense with a polynomial model, as it is impossible for an independent variable to change its value while its *powers* are held constant. So, one must interpret regression coefficients for polynomial models by describing the slope of the relationship (and how it changes) over key ranges in the value of the conceptual independent variable. For example, one useful statement describes the values of the independent variable over which the mean of Y increases as the independent variable increases, and the mean of Y decreases as the independent variable increases. For a polynomial model of order 2

$$Y = \alpha + \beta_1 X_1 + \beta_2 X_1^2 + \epsilon \qquad [5.10]$$

the slope of the curve at any specific value of X_1—say X_1'—can be determined by the formula[11]

$$\text{slope at } X_1' = \beta_1 + 2\beta_2 X_1' \qquad [5.11]$$

Given this, one can easily solve for the value of the independent variable at which the slope equals zero:

$$0 = \beta_1 + 2\beta_2 X_1' \qquad [5.12]$$

This implies that for the model of order 2, the slope of the relationship equals zero at the value of X_1 equal to $-\beta_1/2\beta_2$. Of course, the value of the independent variable at which the slope equals zero is precisely the value at which the curve "bends" from positive slope to negative slope, or vice versa.

For an example of a polynomial model, we examine Hibbs's (1973) analysis of the relationship between economic development and domestic instability. Hibbs argues that domestic violence should increase across nations from low to middle levels of economic development but decrease from middle to high levels, as a result of the affluence accompanying high levels of industrialization. Thus, the slope of the relationship between level of development and level of domestic violence should be positive at low to middle ranges of development but negative at higher ranges. Hibbs specifies this hypothesis using a polynomial model of order 2. He also includes population as an independent variable hypothesized to be linearly and positively related to the level of violence. Then, measuring level of domestic violence by a composite index of collective protest (Hibbs, 1973, Chap. 2) and economic development by the natural logarithm of energy consumption (in ten million metric tons of coal equivalents) per capita, he uses OLS regression to obtain the following coefficient estimates:

$$\dot{Y} = -7.06 + 1.76X_1 - .151X_1^2 + .627X_3 \qquad [5.13]$$
$$\phantom{\dot{Y} = -7.06 + }(.53) \quad\ \ (.048) \quad\ (.13)$$

where Y = level of domestic violence, X_1 = level of economic development, X_3 = population, and the values in parentheses are standard errors of the partial slope coefficient estimates. Analysis of these coefficients (using formula 5.12) shows that the curve expressing the relationship between X_1 and Y has slope zero at $X_1 = -1.76/2(-.151) = 5.83$. This suggests that nations having a value of 5.83 on the measure of economic development can be expected to have the greatest amounts of domestic violence, with violence and development positively related below 5.83, and negatively related above 5.83.

The exponential model. Other nonlinear specifications are appropriate when the slope of the curve representing the relationship between X and E(Y) never changes sign, but increases or decreases in magnitude as the value of X changes. One such specification is an *exponential* model of the form

$$Y = \alpha X^\beta \epsilon \qquad [5.14]$$

Such models—when graphed—take the form of a curve that passes through the origin (i.e., the point X = 0, Y = 0) and has a slope that gradually either increases or decreases in magnitude depending on the value of β [see Figure 5.3(c)]. If β is *greater* than 1.00, the slope *increases* as X increases; if β is *less* than 1.00, the slope *decreases* as X increases. In particular, one can demonstrate with calculus that the slope of this exponential model at any value, X′, of X is given by the formula

$$\text{slope at } X' = \alpha\beta(X')^{\beta-1} = \beta Y'/X' \qquad [5.15]$$

where $Y' = \alpha X'^\beta$. This implies that—in contrast to a linear relationship between X and E(Y) in which every unit increase in X is associated with a constant change in E(Y)—every one *percent* increase in X is associated with a constant *percentage* change in the mean value of Y. Economists generally refer to the percentage change in E(Y) associated with a one percent increase in X as the *elasticity* of E(Y) with respect to X. Thus the model of equation 5.14 is one with constant elasticity of E(Y) with respect to X. In particular, the elasticity of equation 5.14 is *β*; every one percent increase in X is associated with a *β* percent change in the expected value of Y.

To estimate the coefficients of equation 5.14, one transforms it by taking the logarithm of both sides:[12]

$$\log Y = \log \alpha + \beta(\log X) + \log \epsilon \qquad [5.16]$$

Following the transformation, the equation is in linear form; and the coefficients can be estimated by regressing log Y on log X using OLS. This generates unbiased estimators of *β* and log α. Finally, the latter can be used to calculate an estimator of α by taking the antilog of the estimator of log α.

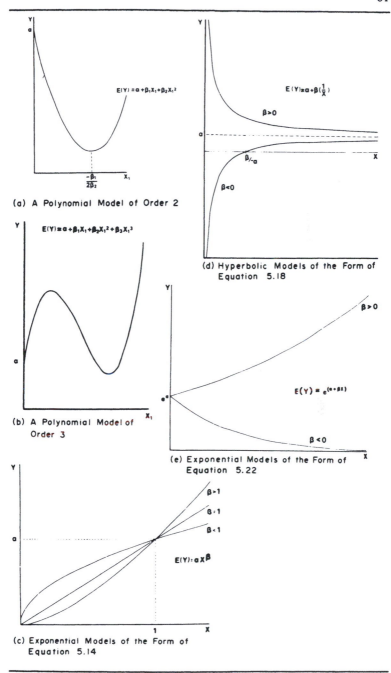

(a) A Polynomial Model of Order 2

$E(Y) = a + \beta_1 X_1 + \beta_2 X_1^2$

$\dfrac{-\beta_1}{2\beta_2}$

(b) A Polynomial Model of Order 3

$E(Y) = a + \beta_1 X_1 + \beta_2 X_1^2 + \beta_3 X_1^3$

(c) Exponential Models of the Form of Equation 5.14

$E(Y) = a X^{\beta}$

$\beta > 1$
$\beta = 1$
$\beta < 1$

(d) Hyperbolic Models of the Form of Equation 5.18

$E(Y) = a + \beta \left(\dfrac{1}{X} \right)$

$\beta > 0$
$\beta / -a$
$\beta < 0$

(e) Exponential Models of the Form of Equation 5.22

$E(Y) = e^{(a + \beta X)}$

$\beta > 0$
$\beta < 0$

Figure 5.3: Illustrations of Nonlinear Models

Note that the assumption made about the error term in exponential model 5.14 is different than the assumption in the basic regression model. In order for the error term in transformed equation 5.16 to take the additive form required for OLS estimation, the error term in the original specification must be *multiplicative*, as in equation 5.14. This means that instead of assuming that the error term in the model has a mean of zero, we assume that the log of the error term has mean zero: for each value of X, $E(\log \epsilon_j) = 0$. This assumption is equivalent to an assumption that for each value of X, the expected *product* of the error terms ϵ_j is equal to 1. This is because in the exponential model, the error term is not the *additive* deviation of Y_j from the mean value of the distribution of Y_j as in equation 1.3; instead the error term ϵ_j is the ratio of Y_j to αX_j^β.

Butler and Stokes (1969) develop an exponential model in a study of the electoral alignment of social classes in Britain. Based on the assumption that individuals perceive and tend to conform to the political norms of their community, Butler and Stokes (1969: 144-150) contend that the greater the proportion of a parliamentary constituency that is middle class (as opposed to working class), the greater the likelihood that a middle-class voter in that constituency will vote for the Conservative party and against the Labour party, and thus the greater the proportion of middle-class voters voting for the Conservative party. Furthermore, they contend that the relationship between the proportion of a constituency that is middle class (to be denoted X) and the proportion of middle-class voters in the constituency voting Conservative (to be denoted Y) should not be linear. The change in Y associated with a constant increase in X is predicted to decrease in magnitude as X increases from 0.00 to 1.00, because once the middle class forms a majority of a constituency, the marginal impact of additional middle-class citizens on the likelihood of a middle-class citizen voting Conservative is fairly small. Based on this expectation, Butler and Stokes estimate the coefficients for an exponential model of the form of equation 5.14 using data from 184 parliamentary constituencies, and derive the following results:

$$\hat{Y} = .97X^{.27} \qquad [5.17]$$

These results provide an estimate of the elasticity of E(Y) with respect to X. Every one percent increase in the proportion of a constituency that is middle class is associated with a .27 percent increase in the expected proportion of middle-class voters voting for the Conservative party.

We can also use equation 5.15 to estimate the slope of exponential model 5.17 at any value of X. For example, the slope at X = .10 is 1.41, whereas the slope at X = .50 is .44. This means that a unit increase in the proportion of a constituency that is middle class is associated with an increase of 1.41 in the proportion of middle-class voters supporting the Conservatives when the constituency is 10 percent middle class, but only an increase of .44 when the constituency is 50 percent middle class.

The hyperbolic model. Another nonlinear specification is a *hyperbolic* or *reciprocal* model. It takes the form

$$Y = \alpha + \beta(1/X) + \epsilon \qquad [5.18]$$

and when graphed, produces a curve in the form of Figure 5.3(d). The most distinctive feature of the hyperbolic model is that as the value of X gets infinitely large, the expected value of Y approaches α. When β is negative E(Y) is always less than α, but approaches α asymptotically from below; when β is positive, E(Y) is always greater than α, but approaches α from above. One can verify this asymptotic behavior by examining the formula for the slope of the curve at a particular value, X', of X:

$$\text{slope at } X' = -\beta/X'^2 \qquad [5.19]$$

Clearly, as X' gets infinitely large, so does the denominator in equation 5.19; thus, as X increases, the magnitude of the slope gradually decreases, eventually approaching zero. The hyperbolic model can be transformed to a model linear in form very easily by defining a variable Z, such that for every observation,

$$Z_j = 1/X_j \qquad [5.20]$$

Then, unbiased estimators of the parameters of equation 5.18 can be obtained by using OLS regression on the model

$$Y = \alpha + \beta Z + \epsilon \qquad [5.21]$$

Another exponential model. A final nonlinear specification takes the form

$$Y = e^{(\alpha + \beta X + \epsilon)} \qquad [5.22]$$

and thus is also called an *exponential* model. As indicated in Figure 5.3(e), this model has a Y-intercept of e^α. When β is positive, the curve has positive slope throughout, but the slope gradually increases in magnitude as X increases. When β is negative, the curve has negative slope throughout, and the slope gradually decreases in magnitude as X increases, with the curve approaching the X axis as Y gets infinitely large. A key characteristic of this type of exponential model is that for any two values of X—X′ and X″—that are a fixed distance apart, the ratio of the associated expected Y values—E(Y′) and E(Y″)—equals a constant value. In particular, if X′ and X″ are a unit distance apart (i.e., X′ − X″ = 1), then

$$E(Y')/E(Y'') = e^\beta \qquad [5.23]$$

Furthermore, when β is positive and small in magnitude (around .25 or less), Tufte (1974: 124-126) has shown that ($\beta \times 100$) is approximately equal to the percentage increase in E(Y) associated with a unit increase in X.

We can transform equation 5.22 to one linear in form by taking the logarithm of both sides to get

$$\ln Y = \alpha + \beta X + \epsilon \qquad [5.24]$$

Then, we can estimate the coefficients of the original model by defining a new variable Z according to the equation

$$Z_j = \ln Y_j \qquad [5.25]$$

and applying OLS regression to the model

$$Z = \alpha + \beta X + \epsilon \qquad [5.26]$$

Dealing with Nonadditivity

The dummy variable interactive model. If a researcher believes that the independent variables in a model interact in influencing the dependent variable, there are several *nonadditive* specifications that are linear and additive in terms of parameters, and thus—following an appropriate transformation—can be estimated using OLS regression. One commonly used interactive specification is called a *dummy variable interactive model*, and is applicable in a situation in which one of the

$$E(Y) = \alpha + \beta_0 X_{(0)} + \beta_1 X_{(1)} + \gamma D$$

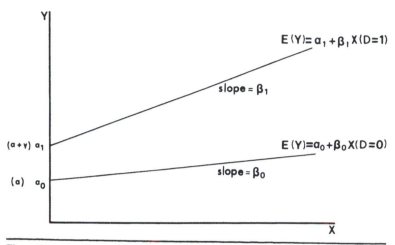

Figure 5.4: An Illustrative Dummy Variable Interactive Model in the Form of Equations 5.27 and 5.28 (or Alternatively, Equation 5.29)

independent variables is *dichotomous* (i.e., has only two possible values). In such a model, a variable X is thought to interact with a dichotomous or dummy variable D in influencing the dependent variable Y as follows: X is linearly related to E(Y) for both values of D, but the slopes and intercepts characterizing the linear relationship differ depending upon the value of D. If we arbitrarily label the possible values D can take on as 0 and 1, then one example of a dummy variable interactive model is graphed in Figure 5.4. In this model, X is linearly related to E(Y) (i) with a slope of β_0 and an intercept of α_0 among the population of cases for which D = 0, and (ii) with a slope of β_1 and an intercept of α_1 among the population of cases for which D = 1.

One way to estimate the coefficients of such a model is through contextual regression analysis. Here, we treat D = 0 and D = 1 as two separate contexts in which we assess the bivariate relationship between X and Y. Thus, we develop two regression equations,

when D = 0: $\quad Y = \alpha_0 + \beta_0 X + \epsilon_0 \qquad\qquad$ [5.27] and

$$\text{when D} = 1: \quad Y = \alpha_1 + \beta_1 X + \epsilon_1 \qquad [5.28]$$

and use OLS regression separately on samples of cases for which $D = 0$ and $D = 1$. Then, the research hypothesis of interaction could be tested against the null hypothesis that $\beta_0 = \beta_1$. A finding that the estimates of β_0 and β_1 differ in magnitude by a substantial amount would be evidence that X and D interact in influencing Y.

We can also estimate the coefficients of the dummy variable interactive model using a single-equation model including the dummy variable as an independent variable. This alternative specification is

$$Y = \alpha + \beta_0 X_{(0)} + \beta_1 X_{(1)} + \gamma D + \epsilon \qquad [5.29]$$

where $X_{(0)}$ and $X_{(1)}$ are variables constructed according to the following rules:

$$\begin{aligned} X_{(0)j} &= X_j \text{ if } D_j = 0, \text{ and} \\ & \quad 0 \text{ if } D_j = 1; \text{ and} \\ X_{(1)j} &= 0 \text{ if } D_j = 0, \text{ and} \\ & \quad X_j \text{ if } D_j = 1 \end{aligned} \qquad [5.30]$$

Let us examine equation 5.29 in the the two contexts ($D = 0$ and $D = 1$) separately. For cases for which $D = 0$, $X_{(1)}$ is also zero, but $X_{(0)} = X$, and thus equation 5.29 reduces to

$$Y = \alpha + \beta_0 X + \epsilon \quad (\text{if } D = 0) \qquad [5.31]$$

In contrast, when $D = 1$, $X_{(0)} = 0$ but $X_{(1)} = X$; thus equation 5.29 takes the form

$$Y = (\alpha + \gamma) + \beta_1 X + \epsilon \quad (\text{if } D = 1) \qquad [5.32]$$

And if we let $\alpha = \alpha_0$ and $\alpha + \gamma = \alpha_1$, equations 5.31 and 5.32 are identical to equations 5.27 and 5.28, respectively (except that equations 5.27 and 5.28 contain different error terms, whereas equations 5.31 and 5.32 contain the same error term). Of course, after constructing the variables $X_{(0)}$ and $X_{(1)}$, the coefficients of equation 5.29 can be estimated using OLS regression, and the estimates obtained would always be equivalent to those obtained using contextual regression analysis; $\hat{\alpha} = \hat{\alpha}_0$ and $\hat{\alpha} + \hat{\gamma} = \hat{\alpha}_1$. The test of the research hypothesis of interaction is also easy to perform. To do so, the analyst must also estimate the coefficients for the additive model in which D and X are the only independent variables

$$Y = \alpha + \beta X + \gamma D + \epsilon \qquad [5.33]$$

using the same data. Then, the null hypothesis that β_0 equals β_1 can be evaluated using the F-test of equation 1.22, where R is the multiple correlation coefficient for the interactive model of equation 5.29, R_m is the multiple correlation coefficient for the additive model of equation 5.33, $k = 2$, and $r = 1$.

The multiplicative model. Another interactive specification is generally called a *multiplicative model*, and is applicable when two independent variables—X_1 and X_2, both measured at the interval level—are thought to interact in influencing Y such that the *slope* of the relationship between each independent variable and E(Y) is *linearly* related to the value of the other independent variable. The specification takes the form

$$Y = \alpha + \beta_1 X_1 + \beta_2 X_2 + \beta_3 (X_1 X_2) + \epsilon \qquad [5.34]$$

We can easily see the specific nature of interaction implied by fixing the value of each independent variable and manipulating terms. For example, assume that we fix X_1 at X'_1. Then, equation 5.34 can be written

$$Y = \alpha + \beta_1 X'_1 + \beta_2 X_2 + \beta_3 X'_1 X_2 + \epsilon \qquad [5.35]$$

Then grouping terms gives

$$Y = (\alpha + \beta_1 X'_1) + (\beta_2 + \beta_3 X'_1) X_2 + \epsilon \qquad [5.36]$$

Similarly, if we fix the value of X_2 at X'_2, and rearrange terms, equation 5.34 takes the form

$$Y = (\alpha + \beta_2 X'_2) + (\beta_1 + \beta_3 X'_2) X_1 + \epsilon \qquad [5.37]$$

Therefore, we can see that when X_2 is held constant at X'_2, the slope of the relationship between X_1 and E(Y) is $(\beta_1 + \beta_3 X'_2)$. So, indeed, the slope of the relationship between X_1 and E(Y)—holding X_2 constant—is linearly related to the value at which X_2 is fixed. Similarly, the slope of the relationship between X_2 and $E(Y)$ (holding X_1 constant) is linearly related to the value at which X_1 is fixed.

The coefficients—α, β_1, β_2 and β_3—of this model have clear interpretations. As usual, the intercept α represents the expected value of Y when both independent variables $(X_1$ and $X_2)$ are equal to zero. Furthermore, if we set $X_2 = 0$ in equation 5.37, we get

$$Y = \alpha + \beta_1 X_1 + \epsilon \qquad [5.38]$$

Thus, we can see that β_1 represents the slope of the relationship between X_1 and $E(Y)$ when X_2 equals zero. In a similar fashion, β_2 can be interpreted as the slope of the relationship between X_2 and $E(Y)$ when X_1 is held constant at zero. What about β_3? It can be interpreted in two ways. From equation 5.37, we see that β_3 equals the amount of change in the *slope* of the relationship between X_1 and $E(Y)$ associated with a unit increase in X_2. For example, when X_2 equals 3, the slope of the relationship between X_1 and $E(Y)$ is $3\beta_3 + \beta_1$. However, if X_2 is increased by 1 unit to 4, the slope increases in magnitude by β_3 units to a value of $4\beta_3 + \beta_1$. Of course, given the symmetry of X_1 and X_2 in the model, a second interpretation of β_3 is the amount of change in the slope of the relationship between X_2 and $E(Y)$ associated with a unit increase in X_1.

The coefficients for the multiplicative model can be estimated by constructing a new variable X_3 according to the formula

$$X_{3j} = X_{1j}X_{2j} \qquad [5.39]$$

and then using least squares regression analysis on the equation

$$Y = \alpha + \beta_1 X_1 + \beta_2 X_2 + \beta_3 X_3 + \epsilon \qquad [5.40]$$

Unless X_1 and X_2 have a correlation of 1.00 (or unless one of the variables is actually a constant), it is impossible that equation 5.40 would be characterized by *perfect* collinearity. But a high degree of multicollinearity is possible; thus analysts using a multiplicative model should test for high multicollinearity using the techniques of Chapter 4.

Analysts should also be warned of an error commonly made in interpreting the coefficient estimates of a multiplicative model. Often, social scientists mistakenly interpret the coefficient estimates b_1 and b_2 as representing the "additive effects" of the independent variables, in contrast to the estimate b_3, which reflects the "interactive effects." But our earlier analysis of the meaning of β_1 and β_2 shows that this interpretation is misleading, and that instead, b_1 and b_2 should be thought of as estimates of "conditional effects"—estimates of the change in $E(Y)$ associated with a unit increase in one independent variable *under the condition* that the other independent variable is equal to zero. Of course, for some models, the substantive meaning of coefficient estimates might be better conveyed by determining the "conditional effects" of one variable when the other is fixed at some *nonzero* value. Indeed, estimates of such conditional effects are easy to obtain for any fixed value of either independent variable. The analyst need only replace the coefficients in equation 5.36 or 5.37 by their respective coefficient estimates, and substitute the "fixed value" of interest for X'_1 or X'_2.

Friedrich (1982) notes that the standard errors of b_1 and b_2 in multiplicative models must also be interpreted with caution, as they too are *conditional* values. Thus, s_{b_1} and s_{b_2} do not reflect the *general* variability of coefficient estimates, but instead the variability of the estimator (i) of b_1 when X_2 is fixed at zero, and (ii) of b_2 when X_1 is fixed at zero, respectively. And in general, when the variables are fixed at *nonzero* values, the variability in estimates will be quite different. Thus, to be meaningful, significance tests of the coefficients in a multiplicative model should be "conditional"; the analyst should determine whether an independent variable has a significant impact on the dependent variable *at a particular value of the other independent variable*. Friedrich (1982) provides appropriate formulas for such conditional significance tests.

Lewis-Beck (1977) develops an interactive model of innovation in Third World organizations that serves as a good illustration of both a multiplicative specification and the use of prior knowledge to help overcome a multicollinearity problem (as discussed in Chapter 4). His model assumes that two factors influence the degree of organizational innovation (to be denoted Y) of Peruvian hospitals: (i) the amount of resources available to the organization (denoted X_1), and (ii) the degree of equality of influence in the organization (denoted X_2). Furthermore, Lewis-Beck hypothesizes that the greater the level of organizational resources, the greater the effect of influence equality on degree of innovation, and similarly, that the greater the equality of influence, the greater the impact of level of resources on degree of innovation. Such a model can be specified by multiplicative equation 5.34.

An attempt to estimate the coefficients of this model using data from 32 hospitals generated severe multicollinearity—certainly not an unexpected problem given the small sample size.[13] But a return to theory about innovation suggested a reasonable a priori expectation that the coefficient β_2—for the influence equality (X_2)—is zero. This is based on the assumption that when organizational resources are totally absent (i.e., $X_1 = 0$), innovation is impossible regardless of the level of influence equality; therefore X_2 has no effect on Y, and β_2 equals zero. If the analyst is willing to accept this assumption, then coefficient estimates for β_1 and β_3 can be derived that are more efficient than those for equation 5.34 by applying OLS regression to the model

$$Y = \alpha + \beta_1 X_1 + \beta_3 (X_1 X_2) + \epsilon \qquad [5.41]$$

A nonlinear interactive model. One final specification of interest is both *nonadditive* and *nonlinear* in nature. It is obtained by modifying the exponential model of equation 5.14 to include a second independent variable:

$$Y = \alpha X_1^{\beta_1} X_2^{\beta_2} \epsilon \qquad [5.42]$$

In this model, the slopes of the relationships between (i) X_1 and $E(Y)$ and (ii) X_2 and $E(Y)$ each depend on the levels of *both* X_1 and X_2. Calculus can be used to determine these slopes at any given values of X_1 and X_2. It turns out that when $X_1 = X'_1$ and $X_2 = X'_2$

the slope of the relationship between

$$X_1 \text{ and } E(Y) = \alpha \beta_1 X_1'^{\beta_1 - 1} X_2'^{\beta_2} \qquad [5.43]$$

Also, because of the symmetry between X_1 and X_2 in the model, the slope of the relationship between X_2 and $E(Y)$ at the same point is $\alpha \beta_2 X_2'^{\beta_2 - 1} X_1'^{\beta_1 - 1}$.

Note that if we hold one of the independent variables in equation 5.42—say X_2—constant, the equation reduces to one of the form of equation 5.14. Consequently, for any fixed value of X_2, the relationship between X_1 and $E(Y)$ reflected in equation 5.42 can be represented by a graph with the shape of that of Figure 5.3(c). Thus, for a fixed value of X_2, when $\beta_1 > 1$, the slope of the relationship between X_1 and $E(Y)$ *increases* as X_1 increases, whereas when $\beta_1 < 1$, the same slope *decreases* as X increases. But in addition, the greater the values of α and X^{β_2}, the greater the amount of change in $E(Y)$ associated with a marginal change in the value of X_1. And because of the symmetry of X_1 and X_2, similar interpretations can be derived for the nature of the relationship between X_2 and $E(Y)$ when X_1 is held constant. Furthermore, just as in the case of the single-variable exponential model, the coefficients β_1 and β_2 can be interpreted as *elasticities*; β_1 is the elasticity of the expected value of the dependent variable with respect to X_1; β_2 is the elasticity of $E(Y)$ with respect to X_2.

The coefficients of the exponential model of equation 5.42 can be estimated by taking logarithms of both sides:

$$\log Y = \log \alpha + \beta_1 \log X_1 + \beta_2 \log X_2 + \log \epsilon \qquad [5.44]$$

This equation is in linear additive form, and thus its coefficients can be estimated by regressing $\log Y$ on the two independent variables—$\log X_1$ and $\log X_2$—to obtain values for $\log \alpha$, β_1 and β_2. One can then get an estimate of α by taking the antilog of the estimate of $\log \alpha$. It is important to note that, just as in the case of the single-variable exponential model, the error term in equation 5.42 is multiplicative; if this assumption is not reasonable, the multivariate exponential specification is inappropriate.

Although all the nonadditive specifications we have examined contain only two "conceptual" independent variables, each model can be easily modified to specify interaction among three or more variables. For example, one could develop an exponential model of the form

$$Y = \alpha X_1^{\beta_1} X_2^{\beta_2} X_3^{\beta_3} \epsilon \qquad [5.45]$$

A researcher using this model, or a modified version of one of the other interactive or nonlinear specifications, should begin by analyzing the specific nature of the interaction or nonlinearity implied by the model. This will involve determining the slope of the relationship between each independent variable and the dependent variable when all independent variables are held constant at specific values. In some cases, this analysis can be done using simple algebra (as with equation 5.33); in other cases, calculus is required (as with equation 5.42).

Some Warnings about Nonlinear and Nonadditive Specifications

Analysts using the nonlinear and nonadditive specifications introduced in this chapter must be attentive to several special concerns. First, as we have seen, some of the models examined contain an additive error term, whereas others contain a multiplicative disturbance term. Indeed, for each specification, the choice about which type of error term to use was determined by which type would allow ultimate estimation with

OLS regression. Of course, this is not a theoretically appropriate criteria for determining the specification of a model. Instead, our knowledge and beliefs about the process being modeled should be the determining factor. At a minimum, analysts using nonlinear and nonadditive specifications should carefully consider whether the assumptions required about the error term are consistent with the situation at hand.

A second concern is to make certain that the transformation used to convert the original model to one in linear/additive form for estimation purposes is defined for all possible values of the variables. Some transformations are simply undefined for certain values. For instance, the logarithm of zero—and that of all negative numbers—is undefined. Thus if a variable to be transformed by taking logarithms could take on the value zero for some cases, the measurement scale for the variable would have to converted before the logarithmic transformation could be applied. In situations where measurement is only at the interval level (and thus the zero point is arbitrary), this would not pose a problem, but if measurement is at the ratio level, an initial transformation to change the zero point would be inappropriate.

Finally, it is common that analysts reporting the results of nonlinear or nonadditive models compare the goodness-of-fit for the model to that of the linear additive model including the same variables. Although it is true that the *expected* (or *mean*) goodness-of-fit for an accurately specified model is better than that for an inaccurately specified model, it does not hold that this will be true for *any sample*. For this reason, we do not think it wise to reject a nonlinear and/or interactive specification in favor of a linear additive one when the former is more theoretically compelling, simply based on a comparison of goodness-of-fit of the two models. Nevertheless, a comparison of R^2 values or standard errors of estimates across two or more specifications can give useful information. But when making these comparisons, one must be careful that the unit of comparison be the same across models. For example, one cannot legitimately compare the error variance for a model in which the dependent variable is measured in untransformed units to that for a model in which the dependent variable is expressed in logarithmic units. Thus, when the dependent variable of a nonlinear or nonadditive model is transformed prior to estimation, one must base a measure of the goodness-of-fit of the model on the size of regression residuals in *untransformed* units. Siedman (1976) outlines a procedure appropriate for comparing the R^2 value for the model of equation 5.14 to that for the linear bivariate regression model including the same variables; the general approach he presents can be modified to be applicable to other nonlinear and interactive specifications.

6. HETEROSCEDASTICITY AND AUTOCORRELATION

We have seen that the multiple regression model requires the assumptions that (i) the mean of the error term equals zero—$E(\epsilon_j) = 0$ for all j, (ii) the variance of the error term is constant so that $VAR(\epsilon_j) = \sigma^2$ for all j (homoscedasticity), and (iii) no autocorrelation is present—the error terms associated with different observations are uncorrelated. In this chapter, we examine the implications of violating these three assumptions relating to the distribution of the error term. We also consider diagnostic tools, and strategies for empirical analysis when the assumptions are violated.

The assumption that the error term has mean zero is generally the least important of the assumptions—and an assumption that, if violated, leads only to minor problems for the analyst. Indeed, even when the error term has a nonzero mean, the *partial slope* coefficient estimates for independent variables remain BLUE. The only effect of a nonzero mean is bias in the estimate for the *intercept* of the model; to be precise, the amount of bias turns out to be the mean value of the error term, as with a nonzero mean for ϵ:

$$E(a) = \alpha + E(\epsilon) \qquad [6.1]$$

Because in most cases analysts are more interested in estimates of the partial slope coefficients for a model, the consequences of violating the assumption that the error term has mean zero tend to be quite minor. In contrast, the effects of violating the assumptions of homoscedasticity and a lack of autocorrelation are more pernicious; thus we devote the rest of the chapter to an analysis of these problems.

When Heteroscedasticity and Autocorrelation Can Be Expected

Heteroscedasticity refers to the situation in which—contrary to the assumption of homoscedasticity—the error term in a regression model does not have constant variance. An example of heteroscedasticity is illustrated in Figure 6.1, which shows the conditional probability distribution of Y for selected values of the independent variable X in a bivariate model. In this case, the variance of the error term—instead of being constant across values of X—gets larger as X increases; the variance of the error term is positively correlated with the independent variable.

There are certain types of situations in which heteroscedasticity is likely to be a problem. One is when the dependent variable is measured

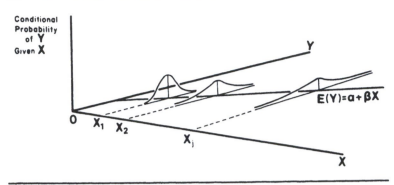

Figure 6.1: An Illustration of a Heteroscedastic Error Term Distribution for a Bivariate Regression Model: $COV[VAR(\epsilon), X] > 0$

with error, and the amount of error varies with the value of the independent variable. For instance, when the unit of analysis is the nation, and data are derived from government records, it may be that some nations keep more accurate records than others. Also, when the unit of analysis is the individual, and data are obtained from surveys, some respondents may provide more accurate answers than others.

Heteroscedasticity is also likely when the unit of analysis is an "aggregate" and the dependent variable is an average of values for the individual objects composing the aggregate units—such as the mean income level in some aggregate unit. If the number of individuals sampled in each aggregate unit to determine the mean income level differs across units, the accuracy with which the dependent variable is measured will also vary; mean income levels estimated from a large sample of individuals will generally be characterized by less measurement error than means based on a smaller sample. This assertion is deduced from knowledge that the variance of the distribution of a sample mean decreases as the sample size increases (Wonnacott and Wonnacott, 1972: 120-122).

Another situation in which heteroscedasticity can be anticipated relates to more substantively meaningful variation in the dependent variable. For example, consider a model in which annual family income is the independent variable and annual family expenditures for vacations is the dependent variable. In this case, it is reasonable to expect that for families with low incomes the mean expenditure level will be low, and variation in expenditures across families will be quite small, as families with low incomes must spend the bulk of their income on

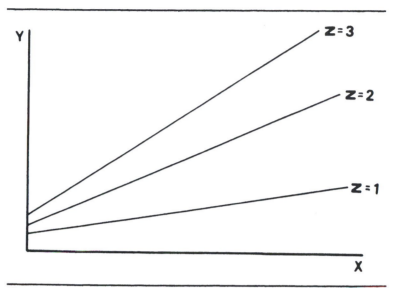

Figure 6.2: An Interactive Model for Which, if Z were Omitted, Regression Residuals Would Have a Similar Pattern to Those for Figure 6.1

necessities thus leaving very few discretionary funds that can be spent on vacations. But as family income increases, the amount of discretionary income should rise, and as a consequence, both the mean vacation expenditure level and the variation in such expenditures should increase—thereby resulting in heteroscedasticity. Note that our expectation about the relationship between income and vacation expenditures could be recast by suggesting that high income is a *necessary but not sufficient* condition for large vacation expenditures. And any time a high value for the independent variable appears to be a necessary but not sufficient condition for an observation having a high value on the dependent variable, heteroscedasticity is quite likely.

In cases in which heteroscedasticity is present and cannot be attributed to measurement error, the problem can often be the result of *interaction* between an independent variable in the model and another variable that has been left out of the model. For example, the heteroscedasticity in Figure 6.1 [with $VAR(\epsilon_j)$ and X_j positively correlated] might be due to interaction between X and some variable Z (not in the model) in influencing Y. One possibility is reflected in Figure 6.2; here, Z is a variable with three possible values—1, 2, and 3. When Z is fixed at any of its values, the relationship between X and E(Y) is linear and the error term is homoscedastic, but the slope of the relationship between X and E(Y) varies depending on the value of Z. In this case, if Z were left out of the model, empirical analysis of the relationship between X and Y would likely produce regression residuals with the same pattern as the model of Figure 6.1.

An analyst examining the relationship between income and vacation expenditures might consider the possibility that the heteroscedasticity present is a result of interaction with a nonincluded variable. One might argue that the amount of a family's expenditure for vacations is determined not only by a family's income, but by the satisfaction its members derive from a vacation. (This is consistent with microeconomic theory, which assumes that one's demand for a good is determined jointly by one's preferences and one's resources). And satisfaction level and income can be expected to interact in determining vacation expenditures; among families that derive little satisfaction from vacations, we can expect income to have a weak effect on vacation expenditures, but as the satisfaction derived increases, income can be expected to have a stronger effect on the level of expenditures.

We can also anticipate factors that would likely result in autocorrelation being present. Recall that we have conceptualized the error term in a regression equation as representing the effects of numerous factors that influence the dependent variable but are not explicitly included in the model. Such omitted factors can result in autocorrelation. The most common situation in which this happens is in time series regression in which the observations consist of a single individual or unit at multiple points in time. Indeed, in a time series model if the omitted factors constituting the error term tend to be the same for each time period, autocorrelation will almost certainly be present.

In this monograph we concentrate on an analysis of heteroscedasticity, and only give brief attention to the problem of autocorrelation. This is not because the latter problem is less important, but because autocorrelation is already discussed extensively in Ostrom's (1978) volume in this series. However, we can note that the major effects of autocorrelation and heteroscedasticity are similar. To preview the complications, the presence of either (i) does *not* result in bias in the OLS estimators of partial slope coefficients, but (ii) does increase their variances. Also, when either is present, the standard errors of partial slope coefficient estimators are no longer unbiased estimators of the true estimator standard deviations. Consequently, tests of statistical significance based on these standard errors will be inaccurate.

Consequences of Heteroscedasticity and Autocorrelation

Let us assume that the error term in a regression model is heteroscedastic, such that

$$\text{VAR}(\epsilon_j) = \sigma_j^2 \qquad [6.2]$$

This means that the variance of the error term may differ in size from one set of values for the independent variables—$(X_{1j}, X_{2j}, \ldots, X_{kj})$—to another. The first question of interest is whether this interferes with the unbiasedness of regression coefficient estimators. And the answer is no; even with heteroscedasticity, the OLS estimators for both the intercept and for partial slope coefficients remain *unbiased*. Thus, on average, OLS slope coefficient estimates are on target even with heteroscedasticity. Furthermore, the same statement applies to least squares estimators when autocorrelation is present.

But with heteroscedasticity—or with autocorrelation—the least squares estimators of the intercept and partial slope coefficients are no longer BLUE, no longer the estimators with *minimum variance* among the class of unbiased estimators. This can be an important consequence given that we typically only have one sample available for estimating the coefficients of a regression model. Each individual OLS estimate has a higher probability of being "off target" than an estimate derived from the unbiased estimator with minimum variance. It turns out that with heteroscedasticity (or autocorrelation), an estimation technique called *generalized least squares* [*GLS*] produces the estimators that are BLUE.[14] Although estimation using GLS is beyond the scope of this book, fortunately, with several specific types of heteroscedasticity, OLS can be modified to develop a procedure called *weighted least squares* [*WLS*] that yields estimates equivalent to GLS estimates, and thus are BLUE.

When we use OLS coefficient estimates to test hypotheses or develop confidence intervals about population coefficients, we must also be concerned with whether the estimates of their variances are unbiased. It turns out that when either heteroscedasticity or autocorrelation is present, the traditional formula used to calculate the standard error of coefficient estimators produces a biased estimator of the true standard deviation of the OLS estimators. For example, with heteroscedasticity in a bivariate regression model, the amount of bias turns out to equal to

$$E(s_b^2) - VAR(b) = \frac{-n(n-1)\left(\sum_{j=1}^{n} x_j^2 \sigma_j^2\right) + (n-1)\left(\sum_{j=1}^{n} x_j^2\right)\left(\sum_{j=1}^{n} \sigma_j^2\right)}{n(n-2)\left(\sum_{j=1}^{n} x_j^2\right)^2} \qquad [6.3]$$

This formula can be used to show that the direction of the bias (positive or negative) is determined by the sign of the correlation between the independent variable and the variance of the error term. If x_j^2 and σ_j^2 are *positively* correlated, the bias in the S_b is *negative*, and thus S_b will tend to underestimate the standard deviation of the OLS estimator, b. This means that confidence intervals for β will be too narrow, and that b may incorrectly appear to be statistically significant when hypothesis tests are conducted. In contrast, when x_j^2 and σ_j^2 are *negatively* correlated, the bias in S_b is *positive*. Consequently, confidence intervals will be too wide, significance tests for b will be too difficult to pass, and the OLS slope coefficient estimator will appear to be less precise than it really is.

Bohrnstedt and Carter (1971) have surveyed a number of studies of the severity of the consequences of heteroscedasticity on tests of statistical significance. They conclude that unless heteroscedasticity is "marked," significance tests are "virtually unaffected," and thus OLS estimation and the associated formula for calculating standard errors can be used without concern of serious distortion. But in some analyses, heteroscedasticity may be severe. We thus turn our attention to procedures for detecting marked heteroscedasticity, and estimation techniques appropriate with severe heteroscedasticity. Although the consequences of autocorrelation are similar to those of heteroscedasticity, diagnosing autocorrelation requires different procedures—those discussed well by Ostrom (1978) and Hibbs (1974).

Detecting Heteroscedasticity

If the analyst suspects marked heteroscedasticity, the first test that should be conducted is a visual inspection of a plot of regression *residuals*. The regression residual for observation j—denoted e_j—is defined as the observation's observed value on the dependent variable

(Y_j) minus its "fitted" value based on the OLS regression equation $(\dot{Y}_j)$:

$$e_j = Y_j - \dot{Y}_j = Y_j - (a + b_1 X_1 + b_2 X_2 + \ldots + b_k X_k) \qquad [6.4]$$

In particular, the analyst should examine a graph in which regression residuals are plotted against the independent variable X_i suspected to be correlated with the variance of the error term.[15] When the sample size is large, homoscedasticity should result in an "envelope" of even width around the horizontal axis when residuals are plotted against any independent variable; such an "envelope" is illustrated in Figure 6.3(a). However, when the sample size is *small*, even with perfect homoscedasticity in the error term, the variance of the regression *residuals* will not be identical at all values of the independent variable. Instead, residuals should be somewhat larger near the mean of the distribution than near the extremes, as illustrated in Figure 6.3(b) (Rao and Miller, 1971); the smaller the sample size, the more magnitude the swelling in the envelope of residuals around the mean. Thus, if it appears that the residuals are roughly the same size for all values of X_i (or, with a small sample, slightly larger near the mean of X_i), it is generally safe to assume that heteroscedasticity is not sufficiently severe to warrant concern. However, if the plot of residuals shows some other type of uneven envelope of residuals, so that the width of the envelope is considerably larger for some values of X_i than others, a more formal test for heteroscedasticity should be conducted. A plot reflecting a case in which the width of the envelope is negatively related to the value of the independent variable is illustrated in Figure 6.3(c).

Goldfield and Quandt (1965) suggest a reasonable formal test for heteroscedasticity in which an independent variable is monotonically related to the variance of the error term—the variance of the error term either increases consistently or decreases consistently as X_i increases. In the Goldfield-Quandt test, one reorders the n observations in the sample in order of increasing magnitude on the independent variable, X_i, suspected to covary with the variance of the error term. Then, one deletes a certain number (denoted m) of "central observations," that is, the middle observation in the ordering plus an equal number of observations above and below the middle one.[16] This leaves n – m observations. Then OLS regression is used to estimate the coefficients of the original model for (i) the first $(n - m)/2$ observations and (ii) the last $(n - m)/2$ observations, separately. If we denote the sum of the squared residuals

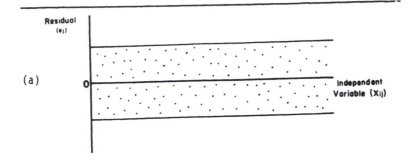

(a)

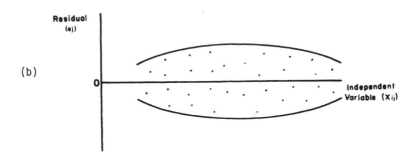

(b)

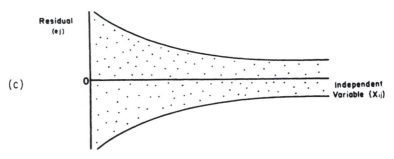

(c)

NOTE: (a) Homoscedasticity with a large sample; (b) Homoscedasticity with a small sample; and (c) Heteroscedasticity.

Figure 6.3: Illustrative Plots of Regression Residuals

for the former regression by ESS_{low}, and the sum of the squared residuals for the latter regression by ESS_{high}, the value

$$F_I = ESS_{high}/ESS_{low} \qquad [6.5]$$

is an F statistic given the null hypothesis that the error term is homoscedastic and the research hypothesis that the variance of the error term is an *increasing* function of X_i; similarly

$$F_D = ESS_{low}/ESS_{high} \qquad [6.6]$$

is an F statistic given the same null hypothesis but the research hypothesis that the error term variance is a *decreasing* function of X_i. Clearly, these F ratios should be approximately 1.00 in value if the error term were homoscedastic. More specifically, both F distributions have $(n-m-2k-2)/2$ degrees of freedom in both the numerator and the denominator (where k denotes the number of independent variables in the model).

Of course, the Goldfield-Quandt test is not helpful if the analyst suspects that there is heteroscedasticity, but not in the form of a monotonic relationship between an independent variable and the error term variance. For example, the test would fail to detect heteroscedasticity in which the error term has small variance at central observations (when the cases have been ordered according to the magnitude of an independent variable) and larger *but equal* variances at the both extremes of the ordering. Glejser (1969) presents a test for heteroscedasticity that involves regressing the absolute values of regression residuals for the sample on the values of the independent variable thought to covary with the variance of the error term. Then the Glejser test for heteroscedasticity involves significance tests for the coefficient estimates from this regression. The advantage of this approach is that one can use a variety of *nonlinear* specifications for the regression of the absolute value of residuals on an independent variable to allow tests for forms of heteroscedasticity in which there is a *non*monotonic relationship between error term variance and the independent variable. Furthermore, the Glejser test can yield an estimate of the specific functional form (whether linear or nonlinear) of the relationship between the variance of the error term and an independent variable. Such information is vital when we seek to obtain estimators for regression coefficients that will have lower variance than the OLS estimators. Details of the Glejser test can be found in Glejser's (1969) original presentation.

An Illustration of Heteroscedasticity:
Income and Housing Consumption

In this section, we consider a regression model

$$Y = \alpha + \beta_1 X_1 + \beta_2 X_2 + \epsilon \qquad [6.7]$$

in which the dependent variable (Y) is the amount of *rent* (in dollars per month) paid by nonrural apartment dwellers. The model includes two independent variables: (i) annual family *income* (in thousands of dollars), to be denoted X_1 and (ii) a dichotomous variable—*community type*, denoted X_2—which takes on the value 0 for central city renters and 1 for suburban renters. We establish as the *"population"* for the analysis a subset (of size 163) of the respondents to a survey of Baltimore and Detroit residents on "economic incentives, values, and subjective well-being " conducted in 1971.[17]

We would expect that families with high incomes would tend to rent higher-cost apartments than families with low incomes, and that suburban housing would tend to be more expensive than central city apartments. Indeed, when data for the full population is used, the OLS partial slope coefficients for both X_1 and X_2 are positive. Specifically, the OLS results showed the following relationship in the "population":

$$Y = 78.70 + 2.74\, X_1 + 16.15\, X_2 + \epsilon \qquad [6.8]$$

But we expect heteroscedasticity in this model; for reasons similar to why we expect heteroscedasticity in the relationship between family income and vacation expenditures, we anticipate that the variance of the error term ϵ (in equation 6.8) should be positively related to total family income, X_1.

We took a random sample of 40 cases from the "population" and estimated the coefficients for the model using OLS regression; the results are presented in column 1 of Table 6.1. To test for the presence of heteroscedasticity, the regression residuals were plotted against family income, X_1, to obtain the graph in Figure 6.4. Inspection of the graph gives clear impressionistic evidence the presence of heteroscedasticity, as the width of the "envelope" of residuals grows steadily in size as income level increases across the sample.

More formal evidence of heteroscedasticity can be obtained from the Goldfield-Quandt test. Following the procedure specified above, we reordered the 40 observations in order of increasing magnitude on X_1; in

TABLE 6.1
Coefficient Estimates for a Random Sample
of Size 40 for Equation 6.7

Population Coefficient	(1) Ordinary Least Squares		(3) Weighted Least Squares	
	Coefficient Estimate (1)	Standard Error (2)	Coefficient Estimate (3)	Standard Error (4)
α	65.57	24.98	89.34	17.57
β_1	4.34	2.70	1.75	2.20
β_2	24.80	14.90	24.21	12.24

this sample, the first case had a value of 4.50, whereas the last had a value of 13.75. Following Goldfield and Quandt's rule of thumb, we deleted the middle quarter of the reordered observations (m = 10), thus leaving 30 cases. OLS regression analysis was then performed for the first 15 and last 15 cases separately, and the sum of squared residuals for the two regressions were $ESS_{low} = 5818$ and $ESS_{high} = 46791$, respectively. Therefore, the F statistic for the null hypothesis of homoscedasticity versus the research hypothesis that the variance of the error term is positively related to X_1 is

$$F_I = ESS_{high} / ESS_{low} = 46791 / 5818 = 8.04 \qquad [6.9]$$

and the degrees of freedom (for both the numerator and denominator) are

$$(n - m - 2k - 2)/2 = (40 - 10 - 4 - 2)/2 = 12 \qquad [6.10]$$

Using a significance level of .001, a table of F critical points (available in most statistics texts) shows that the critical point for 12 degrees of freedom in both the numerator and denominator is approximately 7.1. Because 8.04 exceeds 7.1, we can reject the null hypothesis that the error term is homoscedastic in favor of the research hypothesis that error term variance and family income are positively related.

We have explained that OLS partial slope coefficient estimators remain unbiased even with pronounced heteroscedasticity. Although we cannot prove that this is so for our illustration, we can demonstrate this property by drawing repeated random samples from our "population," and examining the average regression coefficient estimates over the set

84

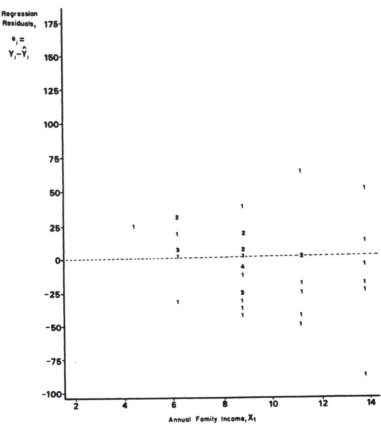

NOTE: Each number on the graph denotes the number of cases falling at a point.

Figure 6.4: Residuals from the OLS Regression Reported in Table 6.1 Plotted Against Family Income (X_1)

of samples. As we have argued above, if an estimator is unbiased, the average value of the estimates obtained over repeated random samples should be very close to the corresponding "population" regression coefficient. In this case, we took 100 different random samples from our population and obtained OLS estimates for each; the results are summarized in Table 6.2. As can be seen, for the intercept α and the partial slope coefficients β_1 and β_2, the average coefficient estimate (in column 2) is quite close in value to the population coefficient reported in

TABLE 6.2
Summary of Results for OLS Regressions for Equation 6.7
for 100 Different Random Samples of Size 40

Coefficient	(1) Population Value	(2) Average OLS Estimate	(3) Column 2 / Column 1	(4) Minimum OLS Estimate	(5) Maximum OLS Estimate	(6) Standard Deviation of OLS Estimates
α	78.70	79.17	1.006	35.23	126.74	22.34
β_1	2.74	2.72	.993	−2.02	8.13	2.50
β_2	16.15	15.32	.948	−5.60	50.82	11.11

equation 6.8 (and reproduced in column 1 of Table 6.2). But although the *average* values of the estimates are "on target," unbiasedness does not ensure that any single estimate will be on target. And, indeed, Table 6.2 shows that the minimum and maximum values of coefficient estimates over the 100 samples are quite far off the mark.

Dealing with Heteroscedasticity and Autocorrelation

If tests indicate the presence of marked heteroscedasticity, the first task of the analyst is to consider the possibility that the heteroscedasticity is a result of interaction of an independent variable with some variable not included in the model. Here, of course, there are no statistical guides; the analyst must rely on theory to suggest potential excluded variables that interact with included variables in affecting the dependent variable. If theory does point to such interaction, dealing with heteroscedasticity becomes a matter of finding the appropriate specification for the type of interaction expected, and estimating the coefficients of the revised model—subjects of Chapter 5. And of course, the consequences of ignoring heteroscedasticity due to "interaction" are quite severe. The proposition that—even with heteroscedasticity—slope and intercept coefficient estimates remain unbiased is correct only under the assumption that the regression model accurately specifies the underlying theory. If the model being tested excludes a theoretically important independent variable that interacts with an included variable, the regression model will misspecify the "true" underlying theory, and coefficient estimates will be biased.

If the analyst can find no basis for expecting that an "interacting variable" has been unreasonably excluded from the model, and is convinced that heteroscedasticity is a result of the nature of measurement of the dependent variable, an aggregated unit of analysis, or other problems, the analyst is free to assume that OLS estimators are unbiased but not BLUE. Attention should then turn to the possibility of using a procedure that yields more efficient estimators. Generalized least squares (GLS) is a technique that will always yield estimators that are BLUE when either heteroscedasticity or autocorrelation is present. GLS accomplishes this by using information about the nature of the relationship between (i) the variance of the error term and an independent variable (with heteroscedasticity), or (ii) the error terms associated with different observations (with autocorrelation). Whereas the OLS criterion requires selecting coefficients that minimize the sum of squared regression residuals

$$\sum_{j=1}^{n} (Y_j - \hat{Y}_j)^2 \qquad [6.11]$$

GLS minimizes a weighted sum of squared residuals. In the case of heteroscedasticity, observations expected to have error terms with large variances are given a smaller weight than observations thought to have error terms with small variances. Specifically, coefficients are selected that minimize

$$\sum_{j=1}^{n} [1/VAR(\epsilon_j)] [Y_j - \hat{Y}_j]^2 \qquad [6.12]$$

This is an intuitively plausible strategy for arriving at estimates more efficient that those generated by OLS; it makes sense that observations with values on the dependent variable, the error component of which is determined by an error term with the smallest variance, should give the best information about the position of the true regression line. However, the use of GLS requires knowledge of the specific nature of the heteroscedastic error term. It is not sufficient to know that the variance of the error term is correlated with a particular independent variable; one must be able to assume a specific functional form for the relationship between the independent variable and the error term variance. The best strategy for determining the appropriate functional form is to rely on theory to anticipate the likely functional form, and then apply the Glejser approach recommended for detecting heteroscedasticity.

A presentation of the GLS estimation technique requires matrix algebra and is beyond the scope of this book (for a good treatment, see Wonnacott and Wonnacott, 1979, Chap. 16). But when heteroscedasticity is present and conforms to one of a few specific "functional forms," estimators equivalent to those generated by GLS can be obtained using a weighted least squares (WLS) procedure utilizing OLS regression on a transformed version of the original regression model.[18]

In the most common application of WLS, the analyst is willing to assume that the standard deviation of the error term is *linearly* related to one of the independent variables. To illustrate the technique, we examine a regression model in which there are two independent variables

$$Y_j = \alpha + \beta_1 X_{1j} + \beta_2 X_{2j} + \epsilon_j \qquad [6.13]$$

and there is heteroscedasticity in which the standard deviation of the error term is linearly related to X_1, for instance

$$SD(\epsilon_j) = k X_{1j} \qquad [6.14]$$

or equivalently,

$$SD(\epsilon_j)/X_{1j} = k \qquad [6.15]$$

where k is a constant. Given this form of heteroscedasticity, the GLS estimates of α, β_1, and β_2 for a specific sample would be the values—a^G, b_1^G, and b_2^G, respectively—that minimize

$$\sum_{j=1}^{n} (1/k^2 X_{1j}^2)(Y_j - \hat{Y}_j)^2$$

It can be shown that we can obtain these GLS estimates by transforming the original regression equation and applying OLS. The transformation required is to divide through equation 6.13 by X_{1j} to obtain

$$Y_j/X_{1j} = \alpha(1/X_{1j}) + \beta_1 + \beta_2(X_{2j}/X_{1j}) + (\epsilon_j/X_{1j}) \qquad [6.16]$$

But given assumption 6.15 about the standard deviation of the error term in equation 6.13, the standard deviation of the error term in transformed equation 6.16 is constant and equal to k. Thus if the analyst constructs three new variables—$Y_j^* = Y_j/X_{1j}$, $X_j^* = 1/X_{1j}$, and $X_j^{**} = X_{2j}/X_{1j}$—OLS regression can be applied to the equation

$$Y_j^* = \beta_1 + \alpha X_j^* + \beta_2 X^{**}_j + (\epsilon_j/X_{1j}) \qquad [6.17]$$

to yield WLS estimates of α, β_1, and β_2. The WLS estimators turn out to be identical to the GLS estimators a^G, b_1^G, and b_2^G, and thus are the estimators of the coefficients for the original model (equation 6.13) that have minimum variance among the class of unbiased estimators.

A similar procedure can be applied to a regression model with any number of independent variables, when it is reasonable to assume that the variance of the error term is linearly related to one of the independent variables, X_i. The first step is always to divide through the original equation by X_i. Then in the second step, OLS regression is used to estimate the coefficients of the transformed equation. The only precaution the analyst must take is to properly "match" the coefficient estimates obtained with the correct independent variables in the original model. For example, note that the intercept of equation 6.17 is *not* the intercept of original equation 6.13; rather it is β_1, the coefficient for X_1 in equation 6.13.

An illustration of WLS. If we are willing to assume that the standard deviation of the error term in equation 6.7 is linearly related to family income (X_1)—an assumption that seems plausible—then WLS can be used to derive regression coefficient estimates which are BLUE. To begin, we divide equation 6.7 by X_{1j}, yielding an equation in the form of equation 6.16. Then, defining the three new variables $Y_j^* = Y_j / X_{1j}$, $X_j^* = 1 / X_{1j}$, and $X_j^{**} = X_{2j} / X_{1j}$, we use OLS regression (with data from the same sample of 40 cases that produced the results in columns 1 and 2 of Table 6.1) to estimate the coefficients of equation 6.17. These estimates are the WLS estimates of α, β_1, and β_2. The results are reported in columns 3 and 4 of Table 6.1. Note that the standard errors of the WLS estimates are smaller than those of the OLS estimates for each of α, β_1, and β_2. This is consistent with the claim that WLS estimators are more efficient than those generated by OLS.

7. ADDITIONAL CONCERNS

In this monograph we have examined some of the major problems that occur when the assumptions of multiple regression analysis are violated. It is not at all uncommon that one or more of the assumptions underlying regression are violated in typical applications. However, this does not mean that a researcher must be content with estimators of partial slope coefficients that are biased or inefficient. In many cases it is possible to anticipate that an assumption may be violated, conduct specific tests of the applicability of the OLS assumptions, and when violated, take some action to deal with the problem and eliminate the bias and inefficiency that often result.

In a short monograph it is not possible to cover every problem that can appear when using regression. But the reader should be aware of several other major issues. First, we have assumed throughout that all of the variables used in a multiple regression analysis are measured at the *interval* level. Using variables measured only at the ordinal or categorical levels violates one of the major assumptions the method is built on. With ordinal or categorical-level dependent variables, alternative estimation procedures such as logit, probit, or discriminant analysis are appropriate (see Hanushek and Jackson, 1977, Chap. 7; Klecka, 1979; Aldrich and Nelson, 1984).

We have also only dealt with *single-equation* models. In many situation, several dependent variables may be examined in a *multi-equation* model, and an independent variable in one equation may be a dependent variable in another. Furthermore, in some cases, "reciprocal causation" between variables may be posited, in which one variable is assumed to be both caused by, and a cause of, a second variable. Multi-equation models such as these require special treatment beyond the scope of this monograph (see Asher, 1983; Berry, 1984; Hanushek and Jackson, 1977).

Finally, we have provided only a basic introduction to more general procedures for estimating models that violate the assumptions of the regression model and make OLS estimation inappropriate. Techniques such as generalized least squares (GLS) and two-stage least squares (2SLS) provide the basis for estimating many more complex models than discussed here. However, a full appreciation of these procedures requires some understanding of matrix algebra (see Hanushek and Jackson, 1977; Kmenta, 1971).

NOTES

1. This is the traditional interpretation of a partial slope coefficient. But the interpretation implicitly assumes that it is possible to manipulate the independent variable, X_i. In many cases in the social sciences this is not possible, especially when the study design is cross-sectional. An alternative way of interpreting a partial slope coefficient is as the expected *difference* in the dependent variable for a one unit *difference* in the independent variable.

2. To be precise, the coefficient estimators will not be 100 percent efficient. From equation 1.13 it can be seen that the standard error of a partial slope coefficient estimator will increase as additional independent variables are added to the model (i.e., as k increases) even if the new variables are uncorrelated with the variables already in the equation. However, as long as the number of cases significantly exceeds the number of variables the increase in the standard error will be trivial.

3. The dependent variable in this model, vote choice (Johnson or Goldwater), is clearly dichotomous. This is technically a violation of the assumption that all the variables in multiple regression analysis are measured at the interval level. Hanushek and Jackson (1977: 205-207) also estimate this model using logit and probit analysis. A discussion of these procedures is beyond the scope of this monograph.

4. The independent variable X_3 is actually the *product* of X_1 and X_2. For a detailed discussion of terms such as this, see Chapter 5.

5. Although the analyst can calculate these R-square values directly with k different regressions, Lemieux (1978) offers a formula for their calculation requiring only the information typically available from a statistical package output for the original regression model.

6. Formulas for this estimator can be found in Kmenta (1971: 385-386); for a more general treatment of the use of external information to improve the estimation of parameters in regression analysis, which relies on matrix algebra, see Goldberger (1964: 255-265).

7. Another approach reasonable when correlated variables are multiple indicators of the same concept is to respecify the model in the form of a multiple indicator model, and estimate coefficients using path analytic procedures (see, e.g., Sullivan and Feldman, 1979) or a maximum likelihood approach such as LISREL (see, e.g., Long, 1983).

8. The elliptical "shape" of the confidence interval results from the negative correlation between the estimators b_1 and b_2.

9. See Kmenta (1971: 461-466) and Cook and Weisberg (1982) for discussions of (i) models that are nonlinear or nonadditive with respect to parameters and, (ii) suitable estimation procedures for such models.

10. This will not necessarily be the case if some of the partial slope coefficients in a model are *precisely* zero. But the number of bends is *always* less than or equal to m-1.

11. The slope of the polynomial model of order 3 at X_1 is equal to $\beta_1 + 2\beta_2 X_1 + 3\beta_3 X_1^2$. Formulas for higher order polynomials can be deterimined using calculus: The slope of the curve at any value of the conceptual independent variable can be determined by finding the derivative of the equation with respect to the variable at that value. Any introductory calculus book should describe this procedure.

12. One can use any base for the logarithms; the most commonly used are base 10 and base e—the latter giving "natural" logarithms.

13. Lewis-Beck does not address the multicollinearity problem specifically in his article; this issue was raised in a discussion with him.

14. When the error term in a model is *homo*scedastic, OLS estimates turn out to be identical to those produced by GLS. (For a good discussion of GLS estimation, see Hanushek and Jackson, 1977: 145-176.)

15. Most computer regression packages—including SPSS and SAS—provide such plots of residuals when requested.

16. In illustrative analyses, Goldfield and Quandt set m to a value corresponding to about 25 percent of the sample size.

17. The data are from ISR (Institute for Social Research, University of Michigan, study 466080). To improve the value of the data set for illustrative purposes, the population was restricted to families with annual incomes less than $15,000. Furthermore, the original data for income are in categories (under $500, $500-$999, $1000-$1999, $2000-$2999, $3000-$3999, $4000-$4999, $5000-$7499, $7500-$9999, $10,000-$12,499, and $12,500-$14,999); the mean values of the categories are used to measure X_1.

18. Readers wishing to use GLS estimation when autocorrelation is present should refer to detailed treatments of the subject by Ostrom (1978) and Hibbs (1974).

REFERENCES

ACHEN, C. H. (1978) "Measuring representation." American Journal of Political Science 22 (August): 475-510.

ALDRICH, J. and F. NELSON (1984) Linear Probability, Probit, and Logit Models. Beverly Hills, CA: Sage.

ALTHAUSER, R. P. (1971) "Multicollinearity and non-additive regression models," pp. 453-472 in H. M. Blalock (ed.) Causal Models in the Social Sciences. Chicago: Aldine.

ASHER, H. B. (1983) Causal Modeling. Beverly Hills, CA: Sage.

BERRY, W. D. (1984) Nonrecursive Simultaneous Equation Models. Beverly Hills, CA: Sage.

BLALOCK, H. M. (1979) Social Statistics (2nd. ed.). New York: McGraw-Hill.

———C. S. WELLS, and L. F. CARTER (1970) "Statistical estimation with random measurement error," chapter 5 in E. Borgatta (ed.) Sociological Methodology. San Francisco: Jossey-Bass.

BOHRNSTEDT, G. W. and T. M. CARTER (1971) "Robustness in regression analysis," pp. 118-146 in H. L. Costner (ed.) Sociological Methodology. San Francisco: Jossey-Bass.

BUTLER, D. and D. STOKES (1969) Political Change in Britain. New York: St. Martin's.

CARMINES, E. G. and R. A. ZELLER (1979) Reliability and Validity Assessment. Beverly Hills, CA: Sage.

FRIEDRICH, C. (1982) "In defense of multiplicative terms in multiple regression equations." American Journal of Political Science 26 (November): 797-833.

GLEJSER, H. (1969) "A new test for heteroscedasticity." Journal of the American Statistical Association 57: 316-323.

GOLDBERGER, A. (1964) Econometric Theory. New York: John Wiley.

GOLDFIELD, S. and R. QUANDT (1965) "Some tests for heteroscedasticity." Journal of the American Statistical Association 60: 539-547.

HANUSHEK, E. A. and J. E. JACKSON (1977) Statistical Methods for Social Scientists. New York: Academic.

HIBBS, D. A., Jr. (1974) "Problems of statistical estimation and causal inference in time series regression analysis," pp. 252-308 in H. L. Costner (ed.) Sociological Methodology 1973-1974. San Francisco: Jossey-Bass.

———(1973) Mass Political Violence. New York: John Wiley.

JOHNSTON, J. (1972) Econometric Methods (2nd ed.). New York: McGraw-Hill.

KLECKA, W. R. (1979) Discriminant Analysis. Beverly Hills, CA: Sage.

KMENTA, J. (1971) Elements of Econometrics. New York: Macmillan.

LEMIEUX, P. (1978) "A note on the detection of multicollinearity." American Journal of Political Science 22 (February): 183-186.

LEWIS-BECK, M. S. (1980) Applied Regression: An Introduction. Beverly Hills, CA: Sage.

———(1977) "Influence equality and organizational innovation in a third-world nation: an additive-nonadditive model." American Journal of Political Science 21 (February): 1-11.

LONG, J. S. (1983) Covariance Structure Models: An Introduction to LISREL. Beverly Hills, CA: Sage.

McADAMS, C. (1984) "The errors in the variables problem in political science data." Presented at the 1984 meeting of the American Political Science Association. Washington, DC.

McIVER, J. P. and E. G. CARMINES (1981) Unidimensional Scaling. Beverly Hills, CA: Sage.

OSTROM, C. J., Jr. (1978) Time Series Analysis: Regression Techniques. Beverly Hills, CA: Sage.

RAO, P. and R. L. MILLER (1971) Applied Econometrics. Belmont, CA: Wadsworth.

SEIDMAN, D. (1976) "Choosing between linear and log-linear models." Journal of Politics 38: 461-466.

SULLIVAN, J. L. and S. FELDMAN (1979) Multiple Indicators: An Introduction. Beverly Hills, CA: Sage.

TUFTE, E. (1974) Data Analysis for Politics and Policy. Englewood Cliffs, NJ: Prentice-Hall.

WARREN, R. D., J. K. WHITE, and W. A. FULLER (1974) "An errors-in-variables analysis of managerial role performance." Journal of the American Statistical Association 69: 886-893.

WONNACOTT, R. M. and T. H. WONNACOTT (1979) Econometrics, 2nd ed. New York: John Wiley.

———(1972) Introductory Statistics (2nd ed.). New York: John Wiley.

ABOUT THE AUTHORS

WILLIAM D. BERRY is Professor of Political Science at Florida State University. He received his Ph.D. at the University of Minnesota, and taught previously at the University of Kentucky. His major substantive areas of interest are public policy, political economy, and state politics. He is author of Nonrecursive Causal Models, *and coauthor of* Understanding United States Government Growth. *He has also published numerous substantive articles and papers about research methodology in such journals as* American Political Science Review, American Journal of Political Science, *and* Journal of Politics.

STANLEY FELDMAN is Professor of Political Science at the State University of New York at Stony Brook. He received his B.A. from SUNY at Stony Brook and his Ph.D from the University of Minnesota. His areas of interest are mass political behavior, political psychology, and methodology. He has published papers on these topics in the American Political Science Review, American Journal of Political Science, Journal of Politics, Political Methodology, *and other scholarly journals and books.*

Made in the USA
Lexington, KY
15 October 2011